FAMOUS DEAD CANADIANS

FAMOUS DEAD CANADIANS

by
Joanne Stanbridge

Illustrated by
Bill Dickson

Scholastic Canada Ltd.
Toronto New York London Auckland Sydney
Mexico City New Delhi Hong Kong Buenos Aires

Scholastic Canada Ltd.
175 Hillmount Road, Markham, Ontario L6C 1Z7, Canada

Scholastic Inc.
555 Broadway, New York, NY 10012, USA

Scholastic Australia Pty Limited
PO Box 579, Gosford, NSW 2250, Australia

Scholastic New Zealand Limited
Private Bag 94407, Greenmount, Auckland, New Zealand

Scholastic Ltd.
Villiers House, Clarendon Avenue, Leamington Spa,
Warwickshire CV32 5PR, UK

Designed by Andrea Casault

National Library of Canada Cataloguing in Publication
Stanbridge, Joanne, 1960-
Famous dead Canadians / Joanne Stanbridge ; illustrations by Bill Dickson.

ISBN 0-7791-1402-7

1. Canada — Biography — Juvenile literature. 2. Canada — History —
Humor — Juvenile literature. I. Dickson, Bill II. Title.

FC25.S73 2003   j971'.009'9   C2003-901058-9
                         F1005.S73 2003

6 5 4 3 2 1   Printed in Canada   03 04 05 06 07

To my family, who give me the Roberts gift of laughter,
the Stanbridge gift of curiosity,
and all the love in the world.

Acknowledgements:

The following people provided help and support far beyond
the call of duty:
Ken Elliott (St. Catharine's, Ontario)
Fred Hammer (Dinosaur Provincial Park, Alberta)
John MacLeod (Fort Malden National Historic Site of
   Canada)
Janet Cobban (Windsor's Community Museum, Ontario)
Clark Bernat (Niagara Historical Society and Museum)
Stu and Sharon Ramsey (Vancouver, B.C.)
Pat Hancock
The staff of the Kingston Frontenac Public Library
Leona Trainer
Sandy Bogart Johnston
and the "High-Test Girls" of Cod Cove Farm

TABLE OF CONTENTS

Introduction viii

Samuel de Champlain's Underwear..........................1

Madeleine de Verchères Stretches the Truth........ 15

Simon Fraser and the Big "Oops" 26

Laura Secord Didn't Make Chocolates 45

Tecumseh Draws the Line 60

John Ware Rides Off a Cliff 77

Louis Cyr and the Bad Advice 91

L.M. Montgomery: Scream! 106

Billy Bishop and the Luck of the Devil 122

Frederick Banting Does his Best 138

Lionel Conacher Does It All 153

"Rocket" Richard: How to Be a Superstar 168

The *Post and Mail* Article 185

Famous Portrait Gallery 187

Illustration Credits 194

Selected Bibliography 196

iNTRODUCTiON

(In which you do not fall into the Niagara River . . . but take a very cool taxi ride instead.)

Can you hear me?

The roar of Niagara Falls is so loud that we'll have to shout! Please don't climb on that railing. The mist has made it slippery, and you might tumble into the river, which is such a horrible thought it makes me feel like hiding my head in a round dark place.

Please gather around and tell me about your school assignment. Answer the following questions by nodding *(Yes)* or shaking your head *(No)*.

1. Did your teacher tell you to learn about a Famous Dead Canadian?

2. Are you supposed to write an essay about this Famous Dead Canadian, including maps or diagrams and a list of interesting books, with bonus marks for neatness and spelling?

3. Did your teacher give you this assignment several weeks ago?

4. Is it due next week?

5. Or tomorrow?

Excellent! You can stop nodding now.

Let me take you on a journey to the homes and haunts of some Famous Dead Canadians. We'll share some laughs, snacks and a little gossip about people who are too dead to defend themselves. Along the way, we'll get your essay written. It will be fun. And painless. I promise.

What did you say? I can't hear you!

You're right. I should have introduced myself. A long time ago, when you were in kindergarten, the newspapers used to call me "the eminent Canadian historian, Professor Plumley Norris." But after **The Incident**, everything changed.

Maybe you've heard grown-ups whispering about my shocking slip of the tongue, but if by some miracle you have not heard about the tragedy, let me just say this: my name is Mr. Norris. I do not teach at the university, or travel the world giving lectures, and it has been a long time since anyone called me eminent. I make my living at the wheel of the big black taxi which is parked in the lot behind you. Once in a while, when desperate students arrive clutching their notebooks and worrying about their assignments, I help them, which makes me feel happy and useful. And that's why I'm so delighted that you will be joining me on one of my patented *Plumley Norris Field Trips and Historical Excursions (Taxicab Edition).*™

Before we go searching for our first Famous Dead Canadian, please take one more look at Niagara Falls. Block out the railing with your thumb. Cover those office buildings with your fingers. Hide those power lines with your other hand and shield your eyes so you won't see the tour boats or the gentleman with his video camera. Now put your eye to the tiny gap between your fingers. You see? That's how Niagara Falls looked about two hundred years ago, before all the Trouble began — just the enormous river thundering over the edge of the cliff, and the beautiful trees and rocks all around. But admiring the Falls will not get your essay written, so let's get moving.

Kindly follow me to the parking lot, and as you climb into the back seat of the big black taxi, please give me your permission slip. You may fold down those little padded benches, which are called jump seats. Please do not jump on them. Just sit down nicely, fasten your seatbelts and put on your very cool sunglasses.

Are you comfortable? Are you buckled in? Are you looking cool? Excellent! Here we go!

Plumley Q. Norris

SAMUEL DE CHAMPLAIN'S UNDERWEAR

My goodness, there's a lot of traffic on this highway! I hope we can find a parking space. Also, I hope we won't drown. We're on our way to the Lachine Rapids, near Montreal, Quebec, and while I can't promise that you'll actually survive this *Plumley Norris Field Trip and Historical Excursion*™, I can pretty much guarantee that you won't die of boredom.

I have a confession to make. Most of the research about Samuel de Champlain is so boring it makes me want to pop my eyeballs out of their sockets and bounce them against the wall. It's just one long list of his comings and goings, hithers and thithers (not to mention his yons.)

For one thing, Samuel spent an awful lot of time sailing back and forth between France and North America. (Pardon me? Oh, I suppose you're thinking I should call someone of his stature Champlain, not Samuel, but I want you to really get to know him. But I wouldn't use *Samuel* versus *Champlain* in an essay you write for school — your teacher might not appreciate it! Thank you — Plumley Norris.) Open any book about him and you'll read something like this: *On August 8, 1610, he departed from Tadoussac, arriving in France around the 27th of September.* A moment later, you're reading this: *On March 1, 1611, he sailed back from France to Tadoussac, arriving around the 21st of May*. And by the time you get to this: *He departed from Tadoussac on July 26, 1618, and was back in France by the 28th of August*, you're ready to burst into tears.

Samuel zipped back and forth so many times you could think that crossing the Atlantic was as easy as a trip to the local doughnut shop — but I assure you it was not. In those days, the ships were small and tubby. They rolled from side to side like crazy while going up and down, up and down on the waves. They didn't have engines, so they relied strictly on windpower, which meant half the time they were sitting with their sails flapping, and the rest of the time they were zooming along like an out-of-control jet plane, usually in the wrong direction. Also, there were storms. And fog. And icebergs. The holds of these ships were horrible, dark and smelly. People got seasick. Sometimes they died. Food rotted. The smell was . . . well . . . Ugh. And the journey across the Atlantic took at least a month. So when Samuel tells us

cheerfully that he made the crossing twenty-one times, feel free to reply with a head-slap and a cry of: "Are you *kidding?*"

Here's what he did when he was in North America: he explored. (This is why he is sometimes called an explorer, which means he showed up in a place which had been inhabited for ten thousand years and allowed the locals to welcome him, take care of him and tour him around.) But trying to read about his explorations is like listening to somebody go on and on about a vacation trip:

> Well, in June I went up the Saguenay River, which was quite exciting. Lots of trees up there. Ever been there? No? You should go sometime. Anyway, a few weeks later I went from Tadoussac to the Lachine Rapids and back to Tadoussac, which was rather fun. Then, in May, I sailed down around the Baie Francaise and explored Port-Royal and we stopped at this place called Sainte-Croix Island, have you ever heard of it? No? Nice place. Cold during the winter, though. The next September – and I think you'll find this interesting –

During his first five years in North America, Samuel's boss was Lieutenant-General François Gravé, Sieur du Pont. And for the next four years he reported to Lieutenant-General Pierre de Gua, Sieur de Monts. Neither of these men was a slouch in the syllable department, and even their short forms — *Du Pont* and *De Monts* — are so much alike to non-French speakers that young researchers might be excused for clutching their heads and moaning "why why why why *why*?"

Ah-HAH — a parking spot! Please lock the doors as you exit the taxi, and stay together as we hurry to the ticket booth.

While we wait our turn I'll tell you something else about Samuel: He made up names for things. Some of the names were wrong, but they stuck. We still use them today. For example, the city of Ottawa was named for some traders from Georgian Bay who just happened to live in the area for a few years, when Samuel met them there. Instead of calling the Innu people by their own name, he called them "Montagnais" because they came from the mountains. And instead of using the real name for the Wendat he called them "Hurons" (which means "boars") because of their hairstyle.

Samuel did most of this naming in French — he didn't speak the native languages. Some of his friends did, though. Young Étienne Brûlé lived (and conversed) with the Algonkin people. And a priest named Père Joseph Le Caron learned the Wendat language. (He had a *teeny* bit of trouble because people kept teaching him the wrong words for things — *rude* words — which he accidentally sprinkled into sermons. For a while, his church was more like a comedy club than a place of worship.) But Samuel lived for thirty-two years among the Algonkin, Wendat and Innu without learning their languages.

Please don't get the wrong idea about him though. Yes, he did sail in a boat with the rather uppity name of *Don de Dieu* (which means "God's Gift"), and he did try to tell the First Nations people how to live, which chiefs to elect, how to worship and so on. But he was an amazingly curious man, eager to learn about everything, and he wrote it all down in books which are much easier to understand than those boring historical surveys I was telling you about. For example, here are a few of his rules for being a good captain:

How to Be a Good Captain: Some Useful Rules
by Samuel de Champlain

(The Short Version, with *Commentary by Plumley Q. Norris*)

1. Be hardy and active.

2. Make sure you have good sea legs. *(If you don't, take them off and throw them overboard.)*

3. Work hard, but pace yourself, so no matter what happens you will be able to appear on deck and give orders to your crew in a loud voice.

4. Make sure that the storerooms are dry and there are plenty of good provisions. *(Including lots of oranges to prevent scurvy. Too bad Samuel didn't know this.)*

5. Go through the daily routine in an orderly manner.

6. Be friendly and soft-spoken in conversation, but give your orders in a firm voice.

7. Punish disobedience severely. *(Samuel once executed a would-be mutineer and displayed the man's head on a spike.)*

8. Encourage good behaviour by being affectionate to people who do a good job and granting them favours. *(And oranges.)*

9. Keep a compass of your own and check it often to make sure that the ship is on the right course.

10. Make sure every person on watch is doing his or her duty. *(And eating his or her oranges.)*

11. Sleep in your clothes, so in case of an accident you can appear on deck quickly. *(Not in your pyjamas.)*

12. If an accident does happen, be brave even in the face of death, and issue orders in a calm voice. *(While eating oranges.)*

I must say, I'm really starting to admire Samuel for that last rule, as we stand here beside the Lachine Rapids. The river is rushing along like a transport truck. Feel that spray on your faces! I'm glad it's not our turn to climb into the rubber raft yet.

At scary times like this Samuel was a real whiz at keeping people's spirits up. For example, after two horrendous winters of starvation and scurvy — not to mention endless, relentless cold — he invented a club called The Order of Good Cheer. Its members took turns throwing parties for each other, stacking the table with great food and wine, and generally having a good time. That was much better than waiting around to drop dead from scurvy.

Soon afterward, he built a fortified settlement called The Habitation, which eventually grew up to be the modern-day city of Quebec. He had a cozy way of making a home for the colonists, and a friendly way of running the place. (Okay, he did execute somebody once and stick the guy's head on a spike, but the man had been planning to murder him!) He also planted rosebushes.

I can't stop staring at the white foam on this river! It's so much more violent than I expected. It reminds me of the summer of 1610, when Samuel stopped here because his boat couldn't get up the rapids.

A year earlier, he had joined his Algonkin, Wendat and Innu friends in a battle against the Haudenosaunee (which many people call the "Iroquois Confederacy"). He did it to seal his friendship with them and to make sure they would stay on his side when trading furs. He felt pretty sure of himself because he had guns and the Haudenosaunee didn't . . . and as predicted, his side won the fight even though they were seriously outnumbered. Samuel killed two enemy chiefs, and then a third. His gun terrified the warriors, who had never seen (or heard!) such a weapon, and it caused a panic. The End.

It was a short battle. But when they fought again the next year, it was harder to win. An arrow went through Samuel's ear into the side of his neck. YOW! He yanked it out and kept fighting (double-YOW!), but that was the last time he and his allies won against the Haudenosaunee.

After the battle, when Samuel was getting ready to leave for France, a teenager in his party (we think it was Étienne Brûlé) kept begging to be left behind so he could spend more time with his Algonkin friends. But in the Algonkin culture, if anything bad happened to Étienne, Samuel would have to fix the balance by taking revenge — and the Algonkin certainly didn't want that! Finally someone came up with the idea of an exchange: a Wendat boy would go with Samuel, and Étienne would stay with Chief Iroquet and his people. Then, at the end of a year (if all went well) they would meet again at the Lachine Rapids and switch back.

So Étienne stayed in North America and had a fabulous time, travelling long distances up the Ottawa River and to the Wendat nation near Georgian Bay. Meanwhile, the Wendat teenager (Samuel called him "Savignon") travelled to France and found that the Europeans were very strange people indeed.

Oh! The group ahead of us is climbing into their raft. Look at them go! Hmm. It's nearly our turn. Are you sure we have to venture into the rapids? Couldn't we just stand here and *look* at them?

Maybe you'll change your mind when I tell you about the horrible thing that happened here in 1611. That's when Samuel came back as planned, to meet up with Iroquet and Étienne and the others. But they weren't here.

He checked his Daytimer™ to make sure he hadn't goofed up the date and then settled down to wait, toodling around in a leaky canoe, touching down at the spot that later became Montreal and making up some more names for things. He found an island which did not yet have any ferris wheels or roller coasters on it and named it Île Ste-Hélène after the bride he'd recently married in France, Hélène Boullé.

Hélène was only twelve years old! Even back in 1610, twelve was just a *teeny* bit too young to get married. So about ten minutes after saying "I do" she went home to her parents' house to finish growing up, while Samuel pocketed three-quarters of the dowry money and came straight back to North America. Did he marry her for the money? Some people say yes. Some say no.

Anyway, Samuel's sightseeing-and-naming spree ended with a terrible shock, right here in this river. One day, Savignon and two friends tried to shoot the rapids, but their canoe flipped over. The other boys drowned, and Savignon struggled back to camp by himself, frightened and exhausted.

The day after the drowning accident, when Samuel went with Savignon to look for the bodies and saw this terrifying place, he said his hair actually stood on end. The rapids were completely white with foam. The noise was like thunder. He couldn't believe the boys had chosen to go through this awful channel when they could have gone another way.

Oh no! Here come our life jackets and helmets. And you

seem to be putting them on quite happily. Didn't that scary story change your minds? No? Then I must be as brave as Samuel.

When he finally met up with Iroquet and safely exchanged Savignon for Étienne, there was an uneasy moment. A bunch of freelance fur traders had followed Samuel to the rapids, and Iroquet's people were (naturally) suspicious of them. They didn't like these uninvited hucksters, and they couldn't help wondering if Samuel had brought them there on purpose. Talking didn't cut it. Samuel wanted to *show* Iroquet's people that he was brave and trustworthy. So he agreed to shoot the rapids himself. In his *underwear*.

Considering that two boys had just drowned here, and considering that Samuel didn't know how to swim and considering that life jackets hadn't been invented yet, this was either incredibly brave or incredibly foolish of him. Men from Iroquet's party stripped down and climbed into eight canoes.

Samuel, feeling shy, kept his undershirt on and tried to look calm while everyone stood around giving helpful advice, like "If there's an accident, hang onto that cross-brace in the middle of the canoe," and "Whatever you do, don't let go."

Samuel's friends must have been amazed and frightened by his boldness. But off he went, riding the crisscrossing waves with his undershirt flapping in the wind. Luckily, no unexpected rocks jumped out to smash his canoe. No sudden currents tumbled him upside down. No gigantic waves swamped him. By the time Samuel finally reached the bottom of the rapids Iroquet's people respected him more than ever. His daredevil performance — which was all in a day's work to them, but not to Samuel — sealed their friendship. Later, he wrote that he had been very nervous. Even the bravest person in the world, he said, would not have been able to do the thing without great apprehension. (He wasn't bragging. That was just a plain fact.)

Later in his life, Samuel did many other brave things. He fought in battles and got badly wounded in the leg by arrows. Once, he got completely lost in the woods by himself for three whole days. Another time, he helped the colonists at Quebec survive for more than a year when they were under siege by the English. He was taken hostage by the English Kirke brothers, who hauled him all the way back to England, found out that the war between France and England had ended, and finally let him go. ("Oops! Sorry!") But in the end none of those adventures killed Samuel. When he was sixty-something years old and living a quiet life in Quebec (doing more gardening and less shooting of rapids) he had a stroke which left him paralyzed. He died on Christmas Day in 1635, in his very own bed.

That may be sad, but it comforts me a little as we lower ourselves into this jiggly rubber raft. Perhaps there's a tiny chance we might survive this adventure and die of old age in *our* very own beds. But first we must be brave, like Samuel de Champlain! Here we go: *EEEEEEEEeeeeeeeee!*

FACTS FACTS FACTS FACTS

Just the Plain Facts about Samuel de Champlain

Note: *this list uses the modern-day names for places (not necessarily what Samuel called them).*

Around 1570
He was born in the seaport of Brouage, France, to Anthoine de Complain and Dame Margueritte Le Roy.

1590 He joined the French Army and fought against Spain.

1599 He left the army and went on several sailing voyages to the West Indies, Mexico and Panama, and to Spanish settlements in North America.

1601 He wrote a book about his voyages, which inspired King Henri IV to send him in search of an ocean route to Asia.

1603 He sailed with Gravé du Pont in a ship called the *Bonne-Renommé.* They visited the St. Lawrence River.

1604–1607 He established settlements in Nova Scotia and New Brunswick. Terrible winters and scurvy killed many settlers. In 1606–1607 Champlain founded The Order of Good Cheer.

1608 Under the direction of Pierre de Monts he established a colony and fur-trading post called The Habitation at Quebec City, the first permanent European settlement in New France.

1609 He made friends with Algonkin, Innu and Wendat people and went on a raid against the Haudenosaunee near Lake Champlain.

1610 Samuel exchanged his young crew member, Étienne Brûlé, for a young man named Savignon. He went to France to obtain money and supplies; while there he married Hélène Boullé.

1611 He returned to the Lachine Rapids to meet again with Iroquet and his other allies, and visited the site of present-day Montreal. He shot the Lachine Rapids in a canoe, and later returned to Quebec and made repairs to The Habitation.

1615 He was wounded in the leg during a battle against the Haudenosaunee, and spent the autumn and winter with the Wendat near Georgian Bay.

1620 His wife joined him in Quebec but she soon became unhappy there and returned to France in 1624.

1627 England and France went to war against each other.

1628 An English fleet, led by five brothers of the Kirke family, cut off supplies to Quebec. After a year, the settlers ran out of food and were forced to surrender.

1629 The Kirkes captured Samuel and took him to England; by the time they got there the war was over, so he was allowed to return to France.

1632 A treaty returned control of the colony to the French.

1633 Samuel sailed back to New France. He was officially put in charge of the fort for the first time, although he was never named governor. He made a number of improvements to The Habitation and started another settlement near Trois-Rivières.

1635 In October Samuel became paralyzed after suffering a stroke. He died on Christmas Day at Quebec City, which at that time was still a small colony of 150 settlers.

1867 A boy found an astrolabe (a navigational tool) dated 1603 near Green Lake, Ontario; it is believed that Samuel may have dropped it when he visited the area in 1613. This astrolabe is now on display in the Canadian Museum of Civilization.

MADELEINE DE VERCHÈRES STRETCHES THE TRUTH

I'm sure she was a perfectly lovely young person, and there is no doubt she was wonderfully spunky, but there is one thing about Madeleine de Verchères which makes it hard for me to tell you about her. She stretched the truth.

Of course, *most* people stretch the truth a *little*. Like this: "Oh *thank you*, Aunt Cecile! I've been *wishing* someone would give me an old-fashioned pickle fork for my birthday!" or "I'd *love* to help you dig the potatoes, but I absolutely must go visit a friend now." But Madeleine stretched the truth a *lot*. She stretched it longer and longer as the years went by. She stretched it to get money. And she stretched it to make a good impression on important people, like governors and countesses.

There. I feel better now. It's one thing to tell the truth so bluntly here in the privacy of our big black taxi. But we're approaching the beautiful village of Verchères, and I would not want to hurt the feelings of its good citizens by insulting their local heroine.

Oh yes, she *was* a heroine. Even if she only did a few of the things she claims, she would still have been heroic. I hope *you* never have to face anything like the terror she faced. And she stretched the truth for a very good reason.

Her family was so poor they were almost starving, and she was under terrible pressure to help them, and if she managed to get a reward by exaggerating a little . . . Well, some people might call that "resourceful." But it certainly doesn't make life easy for historians, as you will find out when you write your essay.

The lovely old building on our left is the *hôtel de ville* — the city hall. As we drive past it and turn the corner onto Madeleine Street, you'll see the green grass of the park stretching down to the river, with masses of brilliant orange and yellow trees all around. No wonder an artist has set up her easel here. What a perfect spot for painting.

Clamber out of the taxi and join me at the foot of that big statue.

Ah. The painter has asked me to pose for her. I hope you won't mind if I hold my chin just so while I tell you about Madeleine de Verchères — this young girl who faces the river so boldly, holding her musket ready, looking very purposeful. No, the real Madeleine was not quite as big as this statue. She was an ordinary fourteen-year-old who lived right here on the south shore of the St. Lawrence River. Her father was a sort of landlord called a *seigneur*. He had been such a loyal soldier that the King of France gave him a section of land, which Madeleine's father rented to local farmers in exchange for a portion of their crops. Her family lived in a big stone house. Nearby were a couple of smaller buildings and a storehouse for food and supplies, and around the whole settlement was a huge fence made of pointed logs, with a high tower at each corner. Beyond the fence lay the fields, and beyond the fields loomed the deep woods.

The real name of this place was Fort Verchères, but its nickname was *Chateau Dangereux*, which means "Castle Dangerous," and when you hear what happened to Madeleine you'll know why.

In 1692 the French and the Haudenosaunee (the French called them *Iroquois*) were at war. Each side had done terrible things to the other. For example, Madeleine's brother-in-law went on a fur-trading expedition and was attacked and killed by the Iroquois. They were retaliating for the deaths of twenty-one Iroquois — who had been killed by the French . . . who had been retaliating for an Iroquois attack . . . which had been in retaliation for a French attack . . . Well. You get the picture. Those were terrifying times. Thank goodness for *Chateau Dangereux*. In 1690, when Madeleine was twelve and her father was away on business, some Iroquois warriors attacked the fort and tried to climb over the walls. Madeleine's mother took charge. The adults scrambled for guns and start-

ed firing at the Iroquois through small holes in the walls of the fort and from the corner towers, which were called bastions. Muskets banged, voices shouted and shrieked, the air stank of gunpowder, and the cannon boomed loudly to warn people up and down the river that *Chateau Dangereux* was living up to its nickname. The warriors ran toward the fort again and again. Again and again the settlers fired at them and drove them away, until night fell and the attack ended. By the time help arrived the next day, the Iroquois had retreated.

Where are you going? Oh, did you think that was the end of Madeleine's heroic deed? No, no, no. We're just getting to that. Please sit down. Here's the set-up:

The Set-Up
Fort Verchères, 1686 – 1692

1. Madeleine's older sister Marie-Jeanne gets married. She is twelve years old.

2. Marie-Jeanne's husband is killed by the Iroquois.

3. She gets married again.

4. While Madeleine's father is away, the Iroquois attack Fort Verchères.

5. Madeleine's brother and brother-in-law are killed by the Iroquois.

6. Madeleine's parents decide to go away, leaving their fourteen-year-old daughter in charge of the fort.

7. What on earth were these people *thinking*?

While Madeleine's father went to Quebec on some military business and her mother went to Montreal to buy supplies for the winter, Madeleine stayed at the fort with a man in his eighties, two soldiers named La Bonté and Galhet, a servant named Laviolette, her two younger brothers, and some of the farmers and their families.

Can't you just smell trouble brewing?

On the morning of October 22, the farmers trooped out to the fields with their rakes and hoes. Dig dig dig. Harvest harvest harvest. Chop chop chop. Madeleine was working in the vegetable garden outside the fort. Meanwhile, the Iroquois were slipping silently through the woods, waiting and watching. Movie music hadn't been invented yet — which is too bad, because the theme from *Jaws* would be perfect right about now.

All of a sudden the settlers started screaming and running. The Iroquois were attacking! The workers in the fields didn't stand a chance. Some warriors grabbed them and disappeared back into the woods. But Madeleine was closer to the fort. She practically flew to the big gate. Later, she claimed that one of the warriors actually grabbed her shawl while she was running, but she escaped by saying a complicated little prayer, untying the shawl as she ran, and leaving him with a handful of cloth. She dashed into the fort and slammed the gate.

Do you remember what I told you in the taxi? About how Madeleine . . . you know . . . may possibly have stretched the truth a *teeny* little bit?

She ran inside and slammed the gate. Women and children were screaming all around her. Most of them had just seen their fathers and husbands being kidnapped. Their shrieking and crying must have made everyone else feel panicky, too, and that kind of fear can make it hard to think or take action.

But Madeleine did think. She did take action. She remembered what her mother had done during the previous attack and she tried to be equally calm and sensible. "*Aux armes!*" she cried. That means, "To arms!" She didn't mean elbows and wrists. She meant "*Grab the weapons!*"

She put on a soldier's hat, ran up the steps into a bastion and fired her musket. Then she ran down and showed herself in another place, and another, hoping she would not look like a fourteen-year-old girl running around shooting a gun, but like a whole troop of fierce and noisy soldiers.

She asked the old man to fire the swivel cannon. What a *boom* that must have made, like thunder, loud enough to shake the ground. Loud enough to warn the neighbours. One by one, each fort fired its own cannon, passing the signal all the way up the river to Montreal.

Meanwhile, Madeleine and the others kept guard, moving around quickly, shooting their guns, and making a lot of noise so it would seem as if the fort was full of people. The warriors had disappeared back into the woods, but as night began to fall Madeleine made a little speech, saying, "God has saved us today from the hands of our enemies. But we must take care not to fall into their snares tonight."

She stayed awake all night long. If you've ever tried that — like maybe the night before a big essay is due — you'll know just how hard it is. An icy wind began to blow, driving wet snow into Madeleine's face. She must have been shivering. Her teeth were probably chattering. But she stayed at her post. All through the night the French called out *"Bon quart!"* ("All's well!") from one part of the fort to another, making sure the guards were alive and awake, and making the Iroquois think there were plenty of soldiers on duty.

Some time during the night the cattle came home. They had run away during the attack, and by the time they got home they were hungry, cold, ready to be milked and surprised to find the gate shut. They mooed. They moaned. They bellowed. Madeleine couldn't leave them outside. But she was afraid to let them in. What if an Iroquois warrior was hidden among them, wearing an animal skin as a disguise? She made her brothers stand by, ready to fire if necessary, as the cows came in. Luckily, the herd turned out to be warrior-free, and the gate was slammed shut again as quickly as possible.

Early the next morning the Iroquois went away with their twenty prisoners, and a few hours later the rescuers arrived from Montreal — fifty Wendat and Algonkin on foot and a hundred French troops in boats. When the French captain entered the fort he must have been very surprised to find an exhausted fourteen-year-old girl wearing a soldier's hat, who offered him her gun and greeted him in the proper military fashion: "*Monsieur, je vous rends les armes.*" Which means, "Sir, I surrender to you my arms." Which, roughly translated, means, "Thanks. Here's my gun. I'm going to bed."

The French soldiers took care of the fort while the Wendat and Algonkin rushed down the Richelieu River to free the hostages. Just imagine how much crying and hugging there must have been when the hostages arrived safely home. (Well, most of them, anyway — two of the prisoners had been killed.) And when Madeleine's parents came home to find their daughter was a hero, did they feel thrilled and relieved and proud . . . and a little bit guilty? Oh yes. I think they did.

And *I* am thrilled and relieved because the artist has finished her painting! Let's see how the picture turned out.

Ah.

Tell the artist which parts you admire the most. The mill? Say, "*le moulin.*" The church in the background? *L'église.* And that little blob that looks like a bug at the foot of the statue? Um, that's me. Say *merci, au revoir,* as the artist leaves us. There she goes. (I did think that portrait might have been just the teeniest bit larger, didn't you?)

It is sad but true that Madeleine's family fell on hard

times. Her father was getting old, the fort was in bad shape and everyone was hungry. Madeleine helped to support her family by hunting deer, but they needed more than that to survive. Seven years after her heroic deed she wrote a letter about it to the Comtesse de Maurepas, who lived in France and hung out with King Louis XIV. The countess and her important friends were impressed with her story, and when Madeleine's father died, his pension money was transferred to her as a reward for her bravery.

Many years passed. Madeleine married a lieutenant and they had five children. When the Governor of New France asked her to tell her story again so he could send it to the royal family, she didn't skimp on the special effects. She told a version that was full of action, excitement and suspense. Probably nobody in the French court cared that it was a bit short on the truth. She said the siege had lasted eight days, not two. She said the fort had been in such bad repair that she was forced to lift some of the great big logs back into place *all by herself*. And she said she left the fort twice — once to escort some neighbours safely past the waiting Iroquois and once to fetch some laundry which had been left on the bank of the river. (Yes, in her new and improved version of the story she risked her life for *laundry*. For *underwear*. Cool!)

No wonder we still remember her. Madeleine may have stretched the truth a little, but she was very brave, and she had a certain flair, and she reminds us what it means to be a real live hero.

Please feel free to go and explore the park now. Visit the mill. Study the statue. Come back whenever you're ready. I'll be right here under this tree. *Vive Madeleine!* Long live Madeleine!

FACTS FACTS FACTS

Just the Plain Facts about Madeleine de Verchères

March 3, 1678

She was born in Verchères, the fourth of twelve children, to François Jarret (a farmer/soldier) and Marie Perrot.

1689 France and England declared war on each other. The Wendat sided with the French and the Haudenosaunee sided with the English.

1690 Madeleine's mother helped to defend the fort for two days during an Iroquois attack.

October 22, 1692
While her parents were away, Madeleine held the fort against an Iroquois attack.

1697 The French and English once again made peace.

1699 She wrote to the Comtesse de Maurepas in France and told her about the incident, hoping to receive a reward which might help the struggling family.

February 26, 1700
Her father died and his pension (of 150 *livres*) was transferred to her.

1701 The Iroquois signed a peace treaty with the French.

September 6, 1706
She married Lieutenant Pierre-Thomas Tarieu de La Pérade and went to live on his *seigneury* on the north side of the St. Lawrence river. They had three sons and two daughters. She and her husband got a reputation for their hot tempers and for treating their tenants badly.

September 1728
Her mother died and was buried at Verchères.

August 1747
Madeleine died at age sixty-nine and was buried under her regular pew at the church in Sainte-Anne-de-la-Pérade.

SIMON FRASER AND THE BIG "OOPS"

Here's one good thing about Simon Fraser: he was very stubborn.

Here's one bad thing about Simon Fraser: he was very stubborn.

One time, Simon decided to canoe to a certain lake and set up a trading post. Nobody could talk him out of it. The journey would have taken just a few days by land, but Fraser was determined to follow the river route. And when he got it into his head to do something, that was that. People started packing the canoes.

As we drive down the Trans-Canada Highway toward Vancouver, British Columbia, our journey is sure to be more pleasant than his!

His 1806 expedition was like one of those awful family vacations where everything goes wrong. The canoes leaked like crazy. They crashed into stumps, rocks, branches and each other. People quarrelled and had accidents and got sick, especially one character called La Malice. The current was so strong they couldn't paddle, but had to grab branches along the river's edge and drag themselves along. That was not exactly the most elegant way to travel, and it was very tiring. Nearly every day they had to pull over to cope with some kind of emergency. But when everyone else's courage failed,

Simon pushed on. He wasn't just stubborn. He was brave. No matter how great the danger, or how terrible the pain and sickness, he quietly and calmly kept going.

Luckily, he had a clever and reliable assistant named John Stuart, who made all the canoes, kept all the records, did all the navigating, and was the only person who could fix anything that got broken. At the end of each day, when the others collapsed near the campfire, Simon and John would scout along the edges of the river, calculate their position, write in their logbooks, take care of the provisions and handle all the problems. They were as tough as their toughest *voyageurs*, and even a little bit tougher, which is really saying something!

But on this trip even the capable John Stuart had trouble. His compass got wet and stopped working. His cloak fell in the water. He left his notebook on a rock and it got knocked into the river. That was too bad, because he could have used it to record the awful things that kept happening, things like this:

The Plumley Norris Rendition of John Stuart's Imaginary Notebook

May 27, 1806

La Malice forgot to tie his canoe and it floated off down the river.

June 1, 1806

St. Pierre had a seizure and collapsed on the shore. La Malice ignored him and went to repair a canoe.

June 19, 1806

Gervais fell out of a tree and seriously hurt an unmentionable part of his body.

June 25, 1806

La Malice got sick.

June 28, 1806

La Malice jumped out of his canoe and fainted on the shore, so we made camp. Saucier is sick. Blais has a lump on his stomach. Lalonde can't steer his canoe.

July 13, 1806

A bear mauled La Garde. The dogs distracted it while he jumped in the river and got away. He had nine or ten bad wounds.

If you've ever experienced a vacation like that, you know how glad the travellers were to reach their destination. And when I tell you that Simon was preparing for an even bigger expedition, you'll join me in exclaiming, "Oh, no! What was he *thinking?*"

What Simon Fraser Was Thinking
(A Handy Checklist)

1. My mission is to find the Columbia, a nice smooth river that will be like a highway to the Pacific Ocean.

2. If we don't hurry, the Americans (like that pesky team of Lewis and Clark) will claim the whole west coast for themselves.

3. I can hardly wait to explore past the point where The Knight* stopped in 1793. *(*Sir Alexander Mackenzie)*

4. I think I'll send La Malice far far far far far *far* away on a time-consuming errand.

5. I wish I could rite and spel better.

What Simon Fraser Was NOT Thinking
(Another Handy Checklist)

1. What if the salmon arrive six weeks late this year, and we starve in the meantime?

2. When exploring a dangerous river, I probably shoud not ask for advice from the people who live there and then do exactly the *opposite* of what they tell me.

3. Since I'm going to the ocean, maybe I should learn something about tides.

4. What if this isn't the Columbia River after all?

5. Maybe Mr. Stuart all reddy has plenty to do without having to copy out my jurnals and fix up my speling.

Do you see the wild river in the bottom of the canyon beside us? Some people call that spectacular. Simon called it "inconceivably dangerous." When he set out from Fort George (which is now called Prince George) with a team of two dozen men and four canoes, they thought they might be able to paddle all the way to the ocean. But this was no ordinary river, and when they started their journey on May 28, 1808, it was swollen from the spring run-off. It was full of whirlpools and rapids, rocks, stumps and broken trees. The people who lived here had one word of advice for Simon: *Don't!*

But you know what he was like.

So he and his men hurtled down this ferocious river, having one scary adventure after another.

Scary Adventure #1
May 30, 1808

Two days into his expedition, Simon tried to impress a group of Lheidli T'enneh people by shooting some guns. One of the guns backfired and injured the man who fired it. The Lheidli T'enneh were certainly impressed.

What did you say? You thought that incident happened when Simon was visiting the Carrier people? The Atnah? The Lhtha-kho-'then? Each of you must have learned this story from a different source.

The communities along Simon's route sometimes have three or four different names:

(1) the name that has been used for thousands of years, long before Simon showed up

(2) that name the way non-native people decided to spell it

(3) that name the way Simon spelled it (believe me, this was one-of-a-kind)

(4) a non-native name, which is often used in books and on maps

If you wrote all those names on a strip of paper, they would look like this:

name **Lheidli T'enneh**	have been called **Lhtha-kho-'then**	Fraser spelled it **Atnah**	have also been called **Carriers**

My goodness, that's a lot to remember. But — how clever of you! By taping the skinny ends of that strip together, you've made a circle, suitable for wearing on your arm. Keep it handy while I tell you about:

Scary Adventure #2
June 1, 1808

Five of Simon's men did an experiment to see whether it was safe to canoe down a certain stretch of the river. It wasn't. The canoe spun around and around in a terrible whirlpool, shot out again, bounced off one obstacle after another and crashed into a rock. The men scrambled out and hung on to the boulder for dear life. Simon and the others slithered down the cliff to rescue them, plunging their daggers into the ground to stop themselves from sliding into the river, and then carving steps into the cliff so they could climb out again.

Scary Adventure #3
June 3, 1808

When the Lheidli T'enneh people couldn't talk Simon
out of his crazy plan to descend the river, they loaned him
four horses to help carry the cargo. One of the horses
promptly tumbled over a cliff. John Stuart's desk and
some of his papers disappeared into the river.
So did the horse. But Simon kept going.

Scary Adventure #4
June 4, 1808

More whirlpools. Somehow the canoes got through without
being swamped or smashed to bits, but the cargo had to be
carried along the cliffs. While inching his way along the rock
face with a large pack on his back, one of the men became
stuck. He couldn't move a muscle without falling to his
death. Simon risked his own life by creeping out along the
ledge. Hanging on by his fingertips, he managed to cut one
of the straps with his knife. The pack crashed down into
the river. Luckily, the man didn't.

Scary Adventure #5
June 9, 1808

The cliffs were so high that if something went wrong there was no way out of the river, and the canoes shot through the canyon like lightning, scaring the you-know-what out of everybody, even Simon, who — as we know — was incredibly brave. Finally he listened to his guides, stashed the canoes and continued the journey on foot. But walking was no picnic either. Everyone was exhausted, and their feet were blistered and full of thorns. They ruined a pair of shoes a day and spent most of their spare time mending or repairing footwear, usually with help from the native people.

After fifteen days of scary adventures Simon's men were thoroughly frightened. Still, he would not give up. He had even named his canoe *Perseverance*! His native guides and interpreters began to go home, slipping away in the night without saying goodbye, or getting sick (or pretending to be sick) so they wouldn't have to risk their lives to help him. Simon was sorry to see them go, but that didn't stop him. He just pushed onward — coaxing, ordering or encouraging his men — doing whatever it took to keep them going. Every day or two they met new people who did not yet know how stubborn (or brave) he was — people who helped him.

At Lytton, twelve hundred Nlaka'pamux welcomed him with singing, dancing and wonderful speeches. (They had a long tradition of generosity to strangers, and besides, some of them thought he was Coyote and had come from the supernatural world.)

Please help yourself to *two* of the special decoder bracelets so you can remember the names of that place and the people who live there:

name Lkamtc'in	sometimes called Kumsheen	Simon spelled it Camchin	on the map Lytton

name Nlaka'pamux	pronounce it Ing-klah-kap-muh	Simon spelled it Hacamaugh	have been called Thompson Indians

Did you think that was the end of Simon's scary adventures? No way.

Scary Adventure #6
June 21, 1808

Some of the men were so footsore and unhappy about walking that they sneaked down to the river and set off in three canoes. What a disaster! The canoes were swamped and the men nearly died. One man got trapped under an overturned canoe that crashed over a small waterfall and broke in half. For three kilometres he went bouncing and swirling down the rapids, clinging to a chunk of broken canoe, until a freak wave picked him up and flung him onto a rock. When Simon and The Boy Wonder (I mean John Stuart) found him, they couldn't believe their eyes. He had somehow managed to struggle up a sheer cliff all by himself. But he was in such bad shape he couldn't even talk.

Scary Adventure #7
June 23, 1808

Now Simon had a different problem. He was ready to canoe down a section of the river in canoes borrowed from the Nlaka'pamux — who, it seems to me, were awfully generous considering what he kept doing to the items he borrowed — but now the men wouldn't go. The near-drowning had scared them so badly they would rather walk. To encourage them, Simon took a heart-stopping gamble with his own life. He climbed into the bow of a canoe and ran down several sets of rapids all by himself. His ploy worked. His show of courage made the others braver. Slowly, over the next few days, they began to follow him again.

But . . . when they got to Hell's Gate, even the brave and stubborn Simon was shocked. Smooth rock walls towered above the churning river, and the only way to get through was to inch along the cliffs, clinging with toes and fingertips. He was amazed by the way the Nlaka'pamux crisscrossed these sheer rock faces, carrying all the gear and encouraging the *voyageurs*, who could not even hold their guns, never mind their heavy packs. His men

crept along in terror. In the steepest places they climbed up and down slender ladders, sometimes leaning backward over the river. In one place they sidled like tightrope walkers along thin poles that dangled over the edge of a cliff.

Just thinking about it makes me dizzy. Let's change the subject while we zoom along these winding roads and through these narrow tunnels. Perhaps you would like to snooze a little as we make our way toward Vancouver.

Zzzzzzzzzzzz

zzzzzzzzzz

Wake up! Surprise! When you nodded off we were gliding along through unspoiled wilderness. Now look where we are. Those houses, shops, roads and buildings across the river are called New Westminster, and just beyond them lies the big city of Vancouver.

Jump out of the cab. You must be eager to stretch your legs. Nowadays this place is all pavement and concrete, so you will have to use your imagination to see it the way it used to be. Picture two Qw'ontl'en settlements. The one on this side of the river was a summer camp called Kikait. On the other side of the river was the main village, called Sxwoyimelth. Here's a bonus double decoder bracelet for you:

name of place Sxwoyimelth	sometimes called Skaiametl	Simon called it "a village"	on the map New Westminster

name of people Qw'ontl'en	it means "tireless runners"	sometimes called Kwantlen	have also been called Langley Indians

Just before lunchtime on July 2, 1808, Simon and his men arrived here at Kikait. Things were not going well. So far the day had gone like this:

Simon Fraser's Bad Day
July 2, 1808

Note: *the times are approximate, but the sequence of events is real.*

4:00 a.m. Simon's men wake up. They discover that some gear has gone missing during the night. They accuse the Qw'ontl'en, and there is a big argument.

4:15 a.m. It turns out the dogs have dragged some of the gear out during the night and a lot of it is wrecked.

5:00 a.m. Simon asks the Qw'ontl'en Chief for the big dugout canoe which had been promised the night before, but the Chief has changed his mind.

5:05–5:15 a.m. Simon and the Chief argue. Simon grabs the canoe. The Chief grabs it back. They each yank at it, and there is an ugly scene, with shouting and threats. Simon scares the Chief into handing over the canoe.

5:16 a.m. Simon's men climb in. The Chief and some others go along, probably to keep an eye on the canoe.

11:00 a.m. Simon tours Kikait and meets the people. But they warn him not to go any farther. They are at war with the people of the islands and along the river west of here, and if Simon ventures too close, he will almost certainly be attacked, and probably killed.

Noon The people do everything they can to prevent Simon from doing such a reckless thing. They pull the canoes out of the water. They beg him to reconsider. Simon ignores them.

12:15 p.m. The people are so distressed, and say such sad and hopeless goodbyes to the Chief, that some of them — including Simon's guides — refuse to go any farther.

12:30 p.m. Simon loads his men and gear back into the hijacked canoe and they keep going. They pick up a new guide along the way.

1:30 p.m. Some Qwon'tl'en men follow Simon's group down the north arm of the river, singing a war song and making angry gestures from their canoes. Even the new guide, who is travelling in Simon's canoe, begins to challenge him, but Fraser threatens him into silence.

We've got one more stop to make. Are you ready? If we hurry, we can get there before the sun goes down. Jump back in the taxi and fasten your seatbelts!

Zzzzzzzzzzz

Here we are. Is there room for another bracelet on your arm? My goodness, you certainly have a lot of them!

name of town & people **X'muthk'i'um**	sometimes spelled **X'muzk'i'um**	Simon spelled it **Misquiame**	on the map **Musqueam**

Step out and walk with me in this quiet place where the crickets are chirping and the grass is blowing. Ahead of us is the Musqueam Reserve. Across the river to our left is a lovely sewage treatment plant. Simon and his men certainly didn't come here to see *that!* They were looking for the place where the river merges into the sea, and when they arrived here they had reached their goal at last.

But there was no cheering and clapping. Nobody did the Happy Dance. In fact, the whole thing turned out to be one big courageous *oops!* from beginning to end.

Simon beached the hijacked canoe, headed up to the village with his men and asked for a tour, bold as you please. When the X'muthk'i'um saw him coming, most of them hurried away into the woods, but a few of the older ones stayed behind. They showed him their beautiful big longhouse and took him through their homes. Then they politely but firmly asked him to go away.

There was only one problem. The tide had gone out while Simon was touring the village, and now the canoe was stranded high on the shore. If you've ever tried to make a smooth but speedy exit only to discover that someone has locked the keys in the car, you will know how he felt. His men grabbed hold of that heavy canoe and dragged it as fast as they could, but they weren't looking very cool or casual while they did it, and the X'muthk'i'um were getting seriously fed up. They rushed out of the woods with weapons and threats. Meanwhile, the Qw'ontl'en who had been following Simon all day closed in, still angry about the hijacked canoe. Everybody was shouting and threatening, and almost everybody had a weapon.

The frantic *voyageurs* launched that canoe and started paddling as hard as they could. Some of them pointed guns at the angry people until the canoe picked up speed and began to move out of range. Later, Simon thought about what might have happened if a shot had been fired, and he realized how close he had come to disaster. Even he shuddered to think what a narrow escape it had been.

He never did see the open ocean. He figured he would go back to Kikait for more supplies and make a return trip the next day. But he and his men antagonized even more people as they went along. They quarrelled with the villagers about missing equipment. They even kicked them, which was such an insult to the Qw'ontl'en men that some of them vowed to kill the *voyageurs*. Soon Simon's group was so busy racing to get away from this new danger that the idea of exploring farther west toward the ocean was abandoned. They turned around and headed back up the river as fast as they could.

Simon probably never knew that he owed his life to a sub-chief named Whattlekainum, who talked some of the Qw'ontl'en men out of killing him. But, oh, how terrible that return journey must have been. By the time he got back to Fort

George (in thirty-five days, which was one day less than he had spent on the journey down the river) some of his men couldn't walk at all, and the rest — including Simon — were limping badly. But it wasn't the physical injuries that hurt the most. In his heart,

Simon was carrying three terrible disappointments:

(1) After all that danger and hardship, he had not seen the open ocean.

(2) The river was so dangerous that it would never be suitable for transporting people and cargo.

(3) The big "Oops." John Stuart's calculations proved that the mouth of the river lay too far north. Simon had realized, at last, that this was not the Columbia River.

He wasn't the type of man to cry into his journal, or to write "Why, why, why?" He simply wrote that if he had known about his mistake he would have turned around before Hell's Gate, way back where he first stashed the canoes. That one little comment tells us he was going home with a broken heart.

The sun is going down on this sad ending. Look at that beautiful shining sky. It makes the brown river look as if it is full of gold. Which, by the way, it was. While Simon and his men were risking their lives on this very river, it was hiding its biggest secret down deep under their canoes. Fifty years later someone discovered it, and almost overnight this valley filled up with people who had just one thing on their minds: Gold.

But that's another story.

Can you guess what this river is called? Of course you can! Here's one last decoder bracelet for you:

name	pronounce it	Simon spells it	on the map
Stó:lo	**Staw-low**	**Columbia River**	**Fraser River**

Just the Plain Facts
about Simon Fraser

1776 Simon Fraser was born near Bennington (which is now in Vermont), the eighth and youngest child of Simon and Isabella (Grant) Fraser. His father was captured while fighting for the British in the American Revolution and died in prison thirteen months later.

1784 After the war ended, American patriots continued to attack the family, so they moved to Upper Canada and settled near Cornwall (which is now in Ontario).

1790 When he was fourteen years old he went to Montreal so he could go to school.

1792 When he was sixteen he became a fur trader/clerk with the NorthWest Company. As an apprentice, he was sent to the northwestern region of what is now Alberta. When he was twenty-five he was promoted and became a partner in the NorthWest Company.

June 1805
His assignment was to find a route (and to build trading posts along it) from the Rocky Mountains to

the Pacific Ocean. It was a daunting task — well suited to someone as stubborn and courageous as Fraser.

Autumn 1805

He built the trading post called Rocky Mountain Portage House on the Peace River, as well as one which would later be called Fort McLeod on Trout Lake (later McLeod Lake). It was the first permanent non-native settlement in what is now British Columbia.

July 1806

He led an expedition to what is now called Stuart Lake and built Fort St. James.

Autumn 1806

He went exploring with John Stuart and built a trading post, which would later become Fort Fraser.

Autumn 1807

At the mouth of the Nechako River, he built Fort George, which would later become Prince George.

May 28, 1808–August 6, 1808

He led his famous expedition down the Fraser River from Fort George to Musqueam and back again.

1810–1815

He took a year off to visit his family, then travelled west again and started a three-year assignment in the Athabaska Department of the NorthWest Company.

August 13, 1816

Though he kept clear of Seven Oaks, he was in the wrong place at the wrong time when the governor of the Red River settlement and nineteen other people were killed during a battle about land rights (now

called the Seven Oaks Massacre). Along with the other NorthWest Company partners, he was arrested for conspiracy, treason and accessory to murder.

August 26, 1816
While he and the other prisoners were being shipped back to Upper Canada for trial, their canoes capsized in a storm near Sault Ste. Marie. Nine men drowned, but he survived.

October 31, 1818
On trial in York (later called Toronto) he was found not guilty of the charges.

June 7, 1820
He settled in St. Andrew's, near Cornwall, Ontario, and married Catherine Macdonnell. Over the next twenty-two years they would have nine children. He made his living as a farmer and owner of two mills.

1837–1838
During the Rebellion of 1837 he served as a captain in the militia which fought against the rebels. On November 7, 1838, he fell and permanently injured his right knee.

1838–1862
Because of the injury, he was unable to walk very well or to take care of his farm or his mills. He was granted a small military pension but lived in poverty for the rest of his life.

August 18, 1862
At the age of eighty-six, he died at his home in St. Andrew's. His wife died the next day without knowing of his death. They were buried together in the same grave.

LAURA SECORD DIDN'T MAKE CHOCOLATES

Get ready for a shock: Laura Secord did not make chocolates. A hundred years after her famous walk (which I will tell you about in a minute) someone borrowed her name for his new candy shop. And the rest, as they say, is history.

Average Canadian person: Laura Secord, eh?
Another Average Canadian person: Yum.

As we drive away from Niagara Falls, please help yourself to a chocolate from the box in the glove compartment. Do you see the little painting on the lid? Please brace yourself for another shock: that is not really a portrait of Laura Secord. It's just a picture of a pretty young woman, invented by an advertising agency to make you think, "Laura Secord, eh? Yum!"

But Laura Secord was a real person, and we are on our way to her house, which is in a town called Queenston, a few kilometres below Niagara Falls.

On your right, you can see the mighty Niagara River rolling along beside us. The trees and rocks on the opposite shore are in the United States. They seem close enough to touch, don't they? Well, in 1812 that was part of the problem. The Americans, who were mad at the British and also possibly a teeny bit eager to get some more land, declared war on England. But England was all the way across a great big ocean, so the Americans just nipped across the border and attacked the conveniently located British colonies right next door. The American president, Thomas Jefferson, said happily, "The acquisition of Canada this year . . . will be a mere matter of marching."

Ha.

If it hadn't been for Laura Secord, you might be pledging allegiance to the Stars and Stripes at school every day. And "Hockey Night in Canada" might never have existed!

Here we are at her home — this small white house with tourists waiting at the door. Let's park here in the middle of Queenston Road.

One Tuesday morning in October, 1812, Laura Secord woke up to the sound of cannons booming. People and horses were running and screaming in the street, this very street where our big black taxi is parked. Gunfire crackled. Shells crashed. And Laura's husband James, a sergeant with the local militia, wasn't home. He was out there in the middle of the danger!

Laura jumped out of bed and ran to save her five children. They dressed as fast as they could. They couldn't go out the front door because of the fighting, so she hurried them out the back and through the fields to a neighbour's house, where they huddled in an agony of suspense. They could hear the explosions in the distance, but there was no way to know what was happening.

Finally, Laura couldn't stand it anymore. She left her children with the neighbour and came back here to the village, where everything was in an uproar. She heard the good news: the American invasion had been stopped. But many American and British soldiers had been killed or wounded. Worst of all, her husband was still lying on the battlefield, badly injured or maybe dead.

Fasten your seat belts, because we're going to rush up the hill to Queenston Heights, just as Laura Secord did back in 1812. Hold on!

Nothing could look less like a battlefield than this beautiful green park with its gardens and its great big monument to Sir Isaac Brock and its small plain monument to Laura Secord. But when Laura got here that afternoon, this field was smoky and dirty and littered with dead bodies. Among the corpses, injured soldiers lay moaning and crying for help. Laura walked among them in a daze.

She found James at last. His shoulder was torn open and a bullet was so deep in his knee that it would be there for the rest of his life. But he was alive! An American officer saw Laura struggling to lift him and came to help. Together they managed to get James all the way back down the hill to the house.

When Laura and James reached their home they discovered that American soldiers had broken into it, stolen most of their things and wrecked the place. Working around the mess, Laura bandaged James's wounds, put him to bed and took care of him. And when I tell you that all of these things happened on October *thirteenth*, I'm sure you will agree that it was an unlucky day for the Secord family.

James would never really be well again, but after it became clear that he was not going to die, life in the Secord home became almost normal. But in June another shocking thing happened. A gang of American bullies nicknamed The Forty Thieves was going around raiding farms and villages, using the war as an excuse to plunder homes and terrorize people. The leader of this gang, Cyrenius Chapin, said he was "protecting the inhabitants from the outrages of the enemy." (Rough translation: *"I'm bullying and stealing from you for your own good."*) By "enemy" he meant the British, because he believed that many of the colonists were sympathetic to the American position and could be persuaded to change sides. But even the American officers couldn't stand him. One of them called Chapin "a vain and boasting liar."

Well, we can't be absolutely sure about this, but we *think* it was Cyrenius Chapin and a couple of his Thieves who burst into the Secord house on Monday, June 21, 1813, demanding something to eat. Laura didn't have much to feed them, but she told the servants, Fanny and Bob, to put everything on the table, because it would not have been smart or safe to resist the intruders. So Fanny and Bob set out a nice meal (which did not include any chocolates, as far as we know, but which did include a few alcoholic beverages) and the

Americans sat down to eat. As they loosened up, their voices got louder and louder. Pretty soon they were bragging. They said they were on their way with 500 soldiers to wipe out the British unit of Lieutenant FitzGibbon and take over the whole Niagara region.

Gasp! Horrors! Why, Lieutenant FitzGibbon was as handsome, kind and modest as Cyrenius Chapin was cruel, vain and dishonest. (At least, that's how we tell it on this side of the border.) FitzGibbon and his men were the only people brave enough to stand up to the Forty Thieves. Just a few weeks earlier, he had saved the day by grabbing a pair of guns from two Thieves with his bare hands. When the British and Canadians cheered and called him a hero, Fitz-Gibbon blushed and waved aside the praise, saying "I acted indiscreetly." (Rough translation: *"Aw, shucks."*) Of course, that just made them love him even more.

So here was Cyrenius Chapin (we think) bragging about his plan, and Laura Secord was listening to the whole thing! What on earth could she do? Please choose the correct answer:

QUIZ

What Could She Do?

1. Jump out and yell, "You'll never get away with it, you scoundrels!"

2. Phone 9-1-1.

3. Get James to crawl 30 kilometres to warn FitzGibbon.

4. Shrug her shoulders, and say, "Hey, it's not my problem. That's why FitzGibbon gets the big bucks."

5. Risk her life by hurrying alone through dangerous territory to the stone house that FitzGibbon was using for his headquarters.

Did you choose #5? Good work!
Have another chocolate!

ㅇㅇㅇㅇㅇ

We don't know whether Laura got much sleep that night. It's generally hard to get a good eight hours on the night before a mission that will (a) push you to the point of physical collapse, and (b) possibly get you killed. But she was up and dressed again at 4:30 a.m. She woke up the older girls, told them she was going to visit their sick Uncle Charles, and asked them to take care of the younger children. Then off she went, wearing a long brown cotton dress with orange flowers on it, a bonnet to shade her from the hot sun, and a pair of soft shoes called house slippers.

THE COW THING

A Plumley Norris Explanation

Average Canadian person: Laura Secord. Yum.
Another average Canadian person: Chocolates.
Yet another average Canadian person: And how about that *cow*, eh?

In 1864, someone* decided to spice up Laura's story by sticking a cow into the middle of it. He said Laura fooled an American sentry by pretending to be a simple farm wife out milking her cow.

BUT THERE WAS NO COW. (In fact, we're pretty sure she didn't see any sentries, either.)

If you unfastened your seat belt during this exciting story, please buckle up again. We're going to retrace Laura's route. Our journey will not be exactly the same as hers, because of course our taxi must stay on the roads, while on that hot day in June, she did her best to stay off the roads for fear of running into American patrols. She preferred to take her chances with the other dangers lurking in the fields and woods.

Footnote: He was an historian called William F. Coffin. He wrote a book that made it seem as if he had interviewed Laura Secord in person. But in the book he kept calling her Mary. Which just goes to show how accurate *his* book was.

Dangers That Lurked in the Fields and Woods

On her journey, Laura knew she might encounter any or all of the following hazards. Please rank them from bad to worst, in order of unpleasantness: rattlesnakes, wolves, heat stroke, bears, skunks, wild cats, exhaustion, dehydration and hostile strangers. Also mud.

Note: Wildcats have been known to hide in trees and pounce on people's heads, screaming, biting, and gouging with their claws. Does *this* information change your answer?

ooooo

As we roll along, please glance out the window at the village of St. David's. Laura stopped here about an hour after she left home, only to discover that her half-brother Charles was still dangerously sick and would not be able to help her. His fiancée, Elizabeth, who was very sweet and delicate and brave and unwell, and maybe just the teeniest bit over-ambitious, decided to walk along with Laura. But when they got to St. Catharine's — in those days it was called Shipman's Corners — Elizabeth had to stop. She was just too tired. The walk didn't kill her, but it probably didn't do her much good, either, and I'm sorry to say that she died the next year.

Anyway, Elizabeth stayed at a friend's house in Shipman's Corners while poor Laura continued on her weary way toward FitzGibbon's headquarters. The walk must have been horrendous. Of course we can't know for sure what Laura was thinking, but I imagine it must have been something like this:

The Plumley Norris Rendition of Laura Secord's Long Walk

Note: this walk is not to scale.

Walk, walk, walk, walk, mud, mud *(it had been raining like crazy)*, mud, mud, mud, walk, walk, walk. Darn, my shoe came off. Walk, walk, walk, walk, mud, mud, walk, walk, walk, walk, mud, mud. Darn, there goes my other shoe. Walk, walk, walk, walk, swamp, swamp, swamp, I hope there aren't any snakes in here. Swamp, swamp, swamp. *Yikes!* What is *that*? Oh, whew, it's just a stick. Swamp, swamp, walk, walk, walk, walk, walk. If I actually live through this, I'll never do another bad thing in my whole life. Walk, walk, walk, walk, I wish I had some chocolates. Walk, walk, walk, walk. I am so hot I could just die. Walk, walk, walk, walk, I am so tired my legs feel like they're going fall off. Walk, walk, walk. I didn't realize how far this was. Walk, walk, walk. Good grief, why didn't I stay home when I had the chance? Walk, walk, walk, walk, walk. Oh, dear, I wish I had never come. But it's too far to turn back now, oh please please please don't let me die. Walk, walk, walk, walk, walk. If I survive this, Lieutenant FitzGibbon will see me in my bare feet. How embarrassing. Walk, walk, walk, walk. Help! It is starting to get dark, and I think I'm lost! Walk, walk, walk. Oh, no, I wish I had

Continued . . .

never come. What was I *thinking?* Walk, walk, walk, walk, walk, walk. I can't believe this. The only way to get across that rushing creek is to crawl along that tree on my stomach. Ow, ow, ow, ow. Please don't let me fall in. Ow, ow, ow, walk, walk, walk. I think I'm lost. Walk, walk, walk. I am so thirsty. Walk, walk, walk, walk, walk, walk, walk. Tired, tired, tired. Look at the size of that hill. Surely I don't have to climb that steep hill NOW? In the dark? I'm so tired I can barely move. And what if I run into a bear? Oh, don't think about bears. Just put one foot in front of the other. Walk, walk, walking, weary, pooped, twigs in hair, walk, walk. Climb, climb, climb. Climb, climb, climb, climb. Climb, climb, climb. Climb. Ow, ow, ow, ow, ow. I don't think I can take another step. Climb, climb, climb. Climb, climb. Climb, climb, climb.

Here at the top of the escarpment — the steep hill which has been making this old taxi groan and complain — let's park and walk for a while. Follow me along this leafy green trail through the woods.

Imagine how exhausted Laura must have felt as she made her way through this forest in the dark. And then, when she was practically at her wits' end, she got another shock. All of a sudden she came upon an encampment of Mohawk warriors. Thinking she might be an American spy, they jumped up and shouted at her, and she was terrified. But slowly it became clear that Laura had an urgent message for Lieutenant FitzGibbon, and that she did not know where to find him. So the Mohawk men led her through the forest to the big stone house where FitzGibbon was staying.

These low stone walls are the ruins of the very house I've been telling you about. We've finally reached Laura's destination, and the best part of her story: she got to go inside the house and *sit down*. Ahhhhhh, how marvellous it must have been to sink into a chair while someone ran to fetch FitzGibbon and a jug of nice cold water. And how thankful Laura must have been when she saw the lieutenant himself and delivered her message at last! Naturally, he thanked her very much for her heroic walk. And then everyone started rushing around, preparing to surprise the Americans.

Here's what Laura did: Rested.

Here's what Cyrenius Chapin did: (1) Said he could guide the American troops to FitzGibbon's house. (2) Couldn't. (3) Got lost.

Here's what the warriors did: hid in the beech woods along the road, waiting for the Americans to pass.

Here's what the Americans did: finally got going in the right direction and marched toward the stone house — these ruins on which you are now sitting.

A couple of kilometres from here, 500 American soldiers were heading up the road. They thought they were sneaking up on FitzGibbon. Ha. As they entered the beech woods a group of Mohawk men slipped out behind them and cut off their retreat. Before the Americans knew what was happening they were surrounded by Six Nations fighters — brave and experienced men who ran dangerously close to them, attacked, melted back into the woods to regroup, and ran close again. The Americans, who knew only how to fight in straight lines, were confused and overwhelmed. After three hours they were exhausted, and still the warriors kept coming.

The battle (now called The Battle of Beaver Dams) was won entirely by the warriors. The British, who stood back and watched, didn't fire a single shot. When the time was right, Lieutenant FitzGibbon came forward and tricked the Americans into thinking he had many more troops than he really did.

Here's what the Americans did: Surrendered.

And Laura Secord rested and rested. Her long walk had been so exhausting that even she could not believe she had really managed it, and Lieutenant FitzGibbon was afraid that the heat and exertion might have damaged her health forever. But on the day after the battle, she went home to her family. (No, *not* walking! Someone gave her a ride. Thank goodness!) The Battle of Beaver Dams was a turning point in the war. If the Americans had destroyed Lieutenant FitzGibbon's unit, the whole Niagara region and maybe even the whole of Upper Canada could have become part of the United States.

But Laura was not a bragging sort of person. And even if she had been, it would not have been wise to boast about her long walk. Her family had already suffered enough trouble, and the last thing they needed was a revenge attack from the

Americans. So they kept quiet about it for many years. Eventually Laura's story began to appear in magazines and newspapers. When she applied for government money because she was so poor, Lieutenant FitzGibbon wrote letters telling about her courageous act. In 1860 the Prince of Wales sent her some gold to say "thank you for your long walk," and that's when Laura really became famous. In 1868, a few months after Canada's first birthday, she died at the ripe old age of ninety-three. And Canadians are still talking about her — the brave and famous Laura Secord, who did not make chocolates.

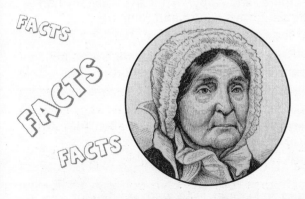

Just the Plain Facts about Laura Ingersoll Secord

September 13, 1775
She was born in Great Barrington, Massachusetts, to Thomas Ingersoll and Elizabeth Dewey.

February 20, 1784

When she was eight years old, her mother died. In 1785 her father remarried, but in 1789 her stepmother died. Later that year her father remarried again.

Autumn 1795

Her family moved to Queenston in Upper Canada. There were eight people in her family at that time: Laura, her father and stepmother, plus her three younger sisters (Elizabeth, Myra and Abigail) her half-brother Charles and two half-sisters (Charlotte and Apollonia).

About 1797

She married James Secord, a Queenston store owner. By 1812 they had five children (Mary, Charlotte, Harriet, Charles and Appy). After the war they had two more daughters (Laura and Hannah).

June 1812

The War of 1812 began and James joined the militia. In October he was wounded at the Battle of Queenston Heights.

April 27, 1813

The Americans captured York (later called Toronto), the capitol of Upper Canada; they burned the Parliament Buildings and other public buildings.

June 22, 1813

She walked 30 kilometres to warn Lieutenant FitzGibbon about an impending American attack.

June 24, 1813

Five hundred Six Nations and Grand River warriors surprised the Americans near Beaver Dams; the Americans surrendered.

August 24, 1814

The British entered Washington, D.C., and burned the Capitol, the White House and other public buildings, an attack that inspired Francis Scott Key to write "The Star-Spangled Banner."

December 24, 1814

The Americans and the British signed a peace treaty called The Treaty of Ghent; all land which had been captured by either side was given up and everything went back to the way it had been before the war.

1835 Laura and James moved a few kilometres upriver to Chippawa, where James became a customs collector.

February 22, 1841

After James died at the age of sixty-eight, Laura was penniless. Her widowed daughter and grandchildren came to live with her. She did needlework and ran a school from her home in order to make money.

1842–1860

Gradually, the story of Laura's long walk became known, and it was published in some magazines and newspapers.

1860–1861

The young Prince of Wales visited Niagara Falls and heard her story; when he got home to England he sent her a gift of £100 in gold.

July 1, 1867

Confederation. Canada's birthday.

October 17, 1868

Laura Secord died at the age of ninety-three.

TECUMSEH DRAWS THE LINE

Are you sure you're supposed to write your essay about Tecumseh? Hmm!

Famous, Dead, Canadian, eh?
(1) Tecumseh *may* be famous (although if you ask a grown-up why, he or she is liable to say, "Um," or "Ah.")
(2) And Tecumseh *is* dead (although nobody knows what happened to his body).
(3) But *no* one, not even your teacher, can say he was Canadian.

It's true that Tecumseh helped the Canadians during the War of 1812 — or, to be more exact, the British. But he wasn't born in Canada. He didn't live here. And if you'd asked him whether he wanted to be a Canadian . . . well, he would have had a few things to say about *that*.

Do you see the Canadian flag flapping over historic Fort Malden here in Amherstburg, Ontario? And do you see the Stars and Stripes fluttering over there on the other side of the Detroit River? Well, Tecumseh risked his life to defend the invisible line which runs down the middle of that river — the border between Canada and the United States. He died defending it. And he never even *wanted* it in the first place. So, we can't really call Tecumseh a Canadian. But since he's such a crucial figure in Canada's history, I'll be delighted to tell you about him.

Let's leave the big black taxi in this parking lot while I tell you about **The Big Handshake** which happened here in 1812. (**The Big Handshake** is one reason some people think of Tecumseh as a Famous Dead Canadian.)

He was a Shawnee chief, born in the territory we now call Ohio. And when he came here to Fort Malden in 1812 he hated the British and Canadians only a *little* bit less than he hated the Americans. He hoped they might treat his people a *teeny* bit better than the Americans did. But he wasn't counting on it. So far, he'd been betrayed or attacked by practically every British or American person he'd met. Nine million Europeans had already settled on the ancient hunting grounds, spreading guns and disease and their strange belief that land could be bought and sold, destroying nations that had existed for thousands of years. Tecumseh wanted a homeland for his people, before it was too late, and he was fighting desperately to get it.

The War of 1812 was about two months old when he and his aides stepped into a room at Fort Malden where Colonel Isaac Brock sat doing paperwork and feeling tired from a stormy voyage down Lake Erie. Isaac and Tecumseh silently sized each other up. Tecumseh wore a beautiful buckskin shirt and leggings. His eyes were full of intelligence, and he walked with dignity. Meanwhile, Isaac looked tall and handsome in his red-and-white uniform. For a second, the needle on the Mutual Admiration Scale hovered around the polite-and-restrained mark. And then — TAH-DAH! — came **The Big Handshake**. A flash of goodwill passed between the two leaders. Isaac said:

(1) I fought for the British king in wars on the other side of the ocean.

(2) I never once backed down from an enemy.

(3) Now I want to fight the king's enemies on this side of the ocean.

(4) I want your men to teach me how to fight in the great forests.

Tecumseh was astonished. He turned to his advisors and exclaimed, "*This* is a *man*!"

Tecumseh had already proven that the British could count on him. A few weeks earlier, when the Americans had boldly crossed the river and tried to capture Fort Malden, he and his warriors had driven them back across the river, raiding an American convoy, stopping the flow of supplies to the fort and capturing the mail.

Okay. Maybe a bag of mail doesn't *seem* like a very valuable prize. But this one contained more than just back-to-school ads and postcards saying:

Hope you're having a nice war.
Don't forget my birthday.
— Love, Snooky.

These letters confirmed that the commander of the American fort, General William Hull, who strutted big and bragged even bigger, actually had a fatal flaw. He was absolutely terrified of being ambushed by native warriors. Ha! So even though Fort Detroit was chock-full of troops, with weapons poised to demolish the British, Tecumseh had a gut feeling about General Hull. He told Isaac to attack the American fort.

Did Isaac answer, "No way, too risky!" or "I'll get back to you next week."? No, he did not. He said, "Tell me more." So Tecumseh drew an excellent map on a sheet of elm bark while Isaac's officers hung over his shoulder saying things like, "No no, that's far too dangerous!" and "You're kidding, right?" But Tecumseh persisted. If you had ever heard him speak (Oh, I wish you *could* — wouldn't that be *amazing?*) you would have been inspired. He was such a gifted speaker that even people who didn't understand his language were impressed by the power and beauty of his words.

At first, only one of Isaac's advisers thought the attack was a good idea. But Tecumseh continued to speak in favour of it. Isaac listened carefully to both sides. Then he made up his mind. Yes. Attack.

The meeting broke up at 4:00 a.m., but nobody got much sleep because it started again the next morning. Isaac and his officers sat under a big oak tree while Tecumseh and his chiefs sat on the grass with a thousand warriors behind them. Everyone listened with great interest because this attack wasn't just to keep Americans from invading Canada. Isaac also wanted to help Tecumseh's people recover land that had been taken away from them by the Long Knives.*

Why Brock Helped Tecumseh
A Peek Inside the Generously-Proportioned Head of Sir Isaac Brock

How would Tecumseh feel if he could gaze into Isaac's brain and see the following thoughts swimming around in there?

1. I want to help Tecumseh's people because their cause is just and it's the right thing to do.

2. I also need Tecumseh's warriors on my side because we're badly outnumbered by the Americans.

3. Also, I like Tecumseh's war strategies, which are like those of a trained British soldier — in other words, he reminds me of *me*.

4. And General Hull is scared of being ambushed by warriors.

5. And a chunk of Indian Territory south of the border would make a nice safe buffer zone between us and the Americans.

6. Besides, I just *like* Tecumseh. *(Mutual Admiration Rating: 12.5)*

Footnote: Tecumseh and his people called the Americans *Long Knives* because of the swords they carried.

So Isaac handed out guns and ammunition to the warriors, and everybody marched up the road to Sandwich* — Tecumseh and his warriors first, then Isaac on his horse, then the British soldiers and militiamen.

Let's climb into the big black taxi and drive up the road about twenty minutes. Along the way, I'll tell you why Tecumseh wanted to fight the Long Knives.

A Few Reasons Why Tecumseh Wanted to Fight the Long Knives

A Plumley Norris Checklist

Reason #1

When Tecumseh was six years old the Americans killed his father. Some say this happened in battle. Others say it happened when Tecumseh's father refused to act as a guide for a group of Americans. It was the first of many sorrows in Tecumseh's life.

Reason #2

His mother went away. His older brother took care of him for three years, teaching him to hunt and fight. Much later, the brother was also killed in battle by American soldiers.

Continued . . .

Footnote: Yes, Sandwich does seem like a funny name for a town. Actually, it was named in honour of the Earl of Sandwich, who had been a British admiral. These days we call it Windsor. (And yes, he was the guy who invented our favourite lunchbox item.)

Reason #3
In 1795 the Shawnee were pushed into signing a treaty that gave the Americans almost their entire territory (a big part of what is now the state of Ohio).

Reason #4
When the Americans forced them out of their traditional hunting grounds, Tecumseh's people could no longer catch enough game to feed themselves. They began to starve. They had to sell more land in order to buy food. That only made things worse, and they were caught in a no-win situation.

Reason #5
Tippecanoe, where Governor Harrison surrounded Tecumseh's village with American troops and burned it to the ground.

Just along here, where the river curves toward Windsor, Tecumseh and 600 of his warriors left the convoy, crossed the river and headed into the woods behind Fort Detroit.

Yes, I know those are skyscrapers, but pretend they're actually a fort with a tall wooden wall around it, gun towers at each corner and, inside, a small town of about 160 buildings plus a few townspeople and a lot of troops.

Tecumseh planned to cut the Americans off from behind.

Imagine how much courage that took. For one thing, he had to get right up close to the enemy. For another, he had to trust Isaac — and as we've seen, he had no reason to trust officers who made promises. But in spite of the danger, he and his warriors positioned themselves behind the fort while Isaac's troops continued up the road to Sandwich.

Do you see this stone house on your left? Yes, it does look lovely and historical now. In fact, it's a museum. But in 1812 it had just been built. It was so new it still smelled of sawdust and mortar. The owner's name was François Baby, and this is called the Baby House.*

As soon as they got here, Isaac's men started building batteries. (Not electric batteries, which hadn't been invented yet, but sturdy structures that could protect, support and aim their weapons.) They built one battery behind an old deserted house and another behind a clump of oak trees. When they were done — TAH-DAH! — they quickly pushed down the house and chopped down the trees. Suddenly General Hull — and Tecumseh, hiding in the woods — saw two rows of guns pointing straight at the front door of Fort Detroit. (Nice dramatic effect, eh?)

Footnote: Please stop giggling. There are no babies in the Baby House. Pronounce it this way: *Baw*–bee House.

While Tecumseh and his warriors waited patiently, Isaac wrote a little note to General Hull. Perhaps it went something like this:

Dear Bill:

How are you? I am fine. Your recent invasions have really been getting on our nerves, so we've decided to take over your fort. Would you like to surrender?

Best wishes to you and your family,
Isaac

General Hull answered something like this:

Dear Isaac:
No.

Sincerely,
Brigadier General William Hull,
Governor of Michigan Territory

So Isaac opened fire on the fort.

Boom, boom, boom! went the shells all night long. They didn't do much damage to the fort, but they made its inhabitants very nervous, especially General Hull, which of course was exactly what Tecumseh and Isaac wanted. Isaac wrote another note — but not to General Hull. It went something like this:

Dear Matthew:

Good news! Five Thousand (5000) warriors have finished capturing the American fort at Michilimackinac and are coming straight here. They'll help us make mincemeat out of everybody at Fort Detroit, especially General Hull. All Five Thousand (5000) warriors will be here any minute. Isn't that great?

See you soon,

Isaac

P.S. Whatever you do, don't let General Hull see this letter!

Isaac made sure General Hull *would* intercept the letter. He was almost finished turning General Hull into a nervous wreck, but he and Tecumseh still had one or two more tricks up their sleeves.

The river isn't visible from the Baby House anymore, but within a block or two we can get a clear view. There. Do you see the Detroit skyline?

It's on the other side of the international border, which runs down the middle of the river. But on August 16, 1812, Isaac and his troops climbed into boats and crossed over without even showing their passports.

On the other side they got together and studied the situation. They decided to play an old but useful trick on General Hull. Isaac ordered his volunteers and militia, who were dressed in their ordinary clothes, as usual, to put on the spare uniforms of the regular troops so it would look as if he had more trained soldiers than he really did. Heh-heh-heh.

Meanwhile, Tecumseh urged his warriors to walk back and forth through the woods within view of the fort, hoping General Hull would peek out. Which he did. He didn't stop to look closely. He didn't say to himself, "Hey, that guy with the scar on his arm has walked past *three* times already!" He thought he saw 5000 warriors gathering in the woods, waiting for the signal to destroy him.

Outside, Tecumseh and Isaac were making plans for serious fighting. Suddenly the gate opened. Out came an officer with a flag of truce and a little message from General Hull:

We surrender.

Isaac and Tecumseh could hardly believe it. They had hoped to make the Americans nervous, but they had never expected such an easy victory. (Neither had Hull's own officers. They were outraged.)

The message went on to say:

Give us three days to make the arrangements.

But Isaac answered:

You've got three Hours, or we'll blow you to smithereens!

Apparently General Hull decided that getting blown to smithereens was almost as scary as being attacked by Tecumseh's 5000 warriors, so the American troops made a speedy exit from the fort and set their weapons on the ground.

Tecumseh and Isaac rode side by side into Fort Detroit and watched the British flag being raised. They captured 2500 American prisoners, many of whom were furious at General Hull for giving up so quickly. After it was all over, Isaac took off his own silk sash and presented it to Tecumseh with a pair of pistols as a thank-you gift. And Tecumseh gave Isaac a valuable wampum belt that became one of Isaac's prized possessions.

The day after the surrender Tecumseh crossed back over the river with his warriors and headed back to Fort Malden for the victory dinner. But before long Isaac had to leave again to head off another American invasion — this time near Niagara Falls. Tecumseh and Isaac said goodbye. They would never see each other again.

On October 13, 1812, when the American troops marched into Queenston and Laura Secord ran out the back door with her children (remember that?) Isaac was on the battlefield with James Secord. And when the fighting was over Isaac lay dead, shot in the chest by a sniper. He never even got to wear the beautiful (and amazingly *large)* hat he had specially ordered from England.

Fast forward to the following October. The war had turned around and the British were in terrible trouble. Tecumseh and his warriors reluctantly joined them in a retreat. The American troops chased them up the road toward Thamesville, Ontario, near a place called Moraviantown. Tecumseh and the British commander finally stopped, turned to face the enemy, and waited.

The battle was over in one horrifying rush. The Americans galloped straight at them, killing forty British soldiers in the first few seconds. The rest of the British troops broke ranks and fled. Their leader (who was a sort of Canadian version of the nervous General Hull) actually passed them as they retreated up the road, leaving Tecumseh with 500 warriors to face about 3000 American troops. The warriors did not stand a chance. In the fight that followed they stood their ground, but the battle was bloody and terrible. And when it was over, Tecumseh was dead.

Nobody knows exactly who shot him (it was probably a militia officer named Colonel Richard M. Johnson, from Kentucky) and his body was never found. Some of the warriors said they buried him secretly in the woods. But to this day, nobody knows where.

Tecumseh's death was a disaster for Aboriginal people. His dreams for a confederacy collapsed, and the British and Americans spread across the whole continent, leaving First Nations people to fight the same battles for years afterward. They are still fighting today — in court, in the media and on the Internet. If Tecumseh had lived, maybe North America would look a lot different today.

Just the Plain Facts about Tecumseh

Around 1768

He was born in the Ohio Valley, probably near present-day Springfield, to a Shawnee chief who may have been called Puckeshinwa. His mother's name was Methoataske. Tecumseh's name is often translated as Shooting Star.

1774 When he was about six his father was killed, so his older brother Cheeseekau took care of him.

August 1794

At the Battle of Fallen Timbers (in present-day Ohio), when the other warriors retreated, Tecumseh charged at the enemy, cut loose their horses and rode away. After promising to help them, the British refused to let the retreating warriors take shelter in the fort.

1795 Tecumseh became a war chief and a band chief. The Treaty of Greenville gave the Americans control of a large part of present-day Ohio, including native hunting grounds. Tecumseh began trying to unite tribes in order to protect land rights.

1808 His brother, The Prophet, became a spiritual teacher.

1809 The Americans again bought a large tract of land from individual tribes (who did not have exclusive rights to it). Tecumseh argued with Governor Harrison of the Indiana Territory, prevented the surveyors from working and threatened the chiefs who had signed the treaty.

1810–1811
He met twice more with Harrison, but the issue was not resolved.

November 7, 1811
While he was travelling in the south, promoting the idea of the confederacy, troops led by Harrison marched on Tecumseh's village at Tippecanoe. They were ambushed by warriors from the village and retaliated by burning it to the ground.

June 1812
Tecumseh went to Fort Malden and offered his support to the British in their conflict with the Americans. The War of 1812 began on June 16.

July 12, 1812
General William Hull led American troops across the Detroit River and invaded Upper Canada, but as they headed for Fort Malden, Tecumseh and his warriors cut them off, chased the Americans back across the river, and ambushed them at Brownstown.

August 13, 1812
Tecumseh met Colonel Isaac Brock at Fort Malden and together they planned an attack on Fort Detroit.

August 14, 1812

They marched to Sandwich, where Tecumseh crossed the Detroit River with 600 warriors and surrounded Fort Detroit while Isaac set up headquarters in the Baby House.

August 16, 1812

After they threatened the fort with their combined forces, General Hull surrendered without a fight.

September 10, 1813

The Americans destroyed the British fleet and gained control of the Great Lakes, forcing the British and Canadians to retreat inland along with Tecumseh and his warriors.

October 5, 1813

Tecumseh and Major-General Procter turned to fight the American force which had pursued them to Moraviantown. The British lines crumbled and Procter retreated. Tecumseh was killed in the following battle. His death marked the end of the native confederacy which he had been struggling to build.

July 23, 1999

In a conference called "Uniting First Nations: Tecumseh's Vision," 4000 First Nations chiefs gathered in Vancouver to discuss ways of strengthening ties across the Canada/U.S. border. It was the largest gathering of First Nations leaders in the twentieth century.

JOHN WARE RIDES OFF A CLIFF

If I tell you the horse's name was Mustard, can you guess what sort of animal it was? Please choose one of the following: (a) spicy (b) hot (c) explosive (d) packed a real kick (e) brought tears to a cowboy's eyes (f) all of the above.

Did you choose (f)? Congratulations! You're right! Like hot mustard, that black gelding *appeared* mild and harmless. You could walk right up to him and stroke his face, and he'd be perfectly happy to see you, as friendly as a dog. But just try to get on his back! You'd soon find out that a little Mustard went a long way!

But there was someone even stronger than Mustard, someone who was just as gentle on the surface and twice as tough on the inside. He was John Ware, Alberta's first black cowboy. And in 1883, when John challenged Mustard, it was nearly the end of both of them!

As we climb out of the taxi and walk across the parking lot, will you pause for a moment to admire my new cowboy boots? Aren't they beautiful?

I thought you'd like them. Now follow me into Alberta's Dinosaur Provincial Park, where the most famous Dead Canadians in the world are fossilized. But we're not here to learn about dinosaurs. John Ware's house just happens to be in this park.

Let's walk up this gravel path to his little log cabin under the cottonwood trees. I hope the sharp stones won't scuff my new cowboy boots.

Look up. Do you see that rough signboard over our heads? No, those are not giant commas or apostrophes. They're four nines — 9999 — the mark John used to brand his cattle. In those days his ranch was on a creek about 20 kilometres from here, but after he died his log cabin was left empty and began to fall apart. Eventually, some people moved it here to the park, fixed it up — and here it is!

If that crazy horse Mustard had managed to kill him, this cabin never would have been built. But something extraordinary happened the day Mustard and John went face to face. (Actually, it was more like butt to saddle.) And it showed what an amazing man John Ware was.

He was out on the range with some other cowboys, rounding up cattle. They set up camp near a cliff, called a cutbank, on the north side of the Old Man River, and Mustard was soon up to his old tricks. When a young cowboy tried to ride him he went into a wild fit of bucking. He smashed the food wagon, spilled the coffee and stomped the flour into the dirt. The young cowboy flew out of the saddle and landed with a thud. Painfully, he got up and tried again. And again. But every time he got into the saddle that ornery horse threw him to the ground. Finally, when the young cowboy was too sore and scared to try again, he swallowed his pride and asked John for help.

John was a big, quiet man with a great sense of humour. Nobody at the ranch was stronger or more skilful than he was. The other cowboys watched while he adjusted the saddle. He and Mustard seemed so relaxed they were practically grinning at each other, but nobody was fooled. They knew what was going to happen. They got out of the way.

Sure enough, as soon as John's rear end touched the saddle, Mustard took off like a firecracker. He bucked and twisted. He roared. He jammed his hooves into the ground. He ran and stopped with a jolt that should have sent John flying over his head. But John stuck to him like Velcro™.

For a few seconds everyone stood around and enjoyed the show. They were amazed at the way John could stay on that whirling horse. But suddenly they began to shout: "John, watch out! Jump off! Get off him!"

John didn't hear them. His whole mind was focussed on the dizzy, jerking ride . . . and Mustard's whole mind was focussed on getting rid of him. Neither of them saw the cutbank. The other cowboys ran forward, frantically waving their arms to turn the horse around. But do you think Mustard paid any attention? No, of course he didn't.

Like a rocket, he blasted right off the edge of the cliff.

And yet . . . you and I are standing here looking at John's cabin, which he built *after* the Mustard Incident, so we know he wasn't killed that day. As John and Mustard shot off the edge of the cliff, they fell straight down. (I know this happens often in the Saturday morning cartoons, but believe me, in real life it hardly ever does!) By some miracle, they plunged the entire six metres right down into the river without twisting, sliding or tumbling. All four of Mustard's hooves hit the water at the same time.

And that wasn't the only miracle. With a tremendous *splash!* the man and the horse disappeared completely under the water. The river just happened to be very deep at that place. If it had been shallow, or if they had landed on the rocks, well . . . ugh.

After the splash there were several long seconds of agonized silence. The cowboys skidded to a halt at the edge of the cut-bank and stared at the place where John and Mustard had gone under. They asked themselves: (a) does John know how to swim? (b) were John and Mustard instantly drowned? (c) were they knocked unconscious? (d) did they get tangled in the reins under the water? (e) all of the above? (f) none of the above?

I'm relieved to say that the answer was, once again, (f) none of the above. A few metres downstream, John's head emerged from the water, and then Mustard's head popped up in front of him.

The cowboys couldn't believe their eyes. John was still in the saddle! He still held the reins! His feet were still in the stirrups! As if he were merely out for an afternoon ride, he steered the swimming horse to a shallower place, urged him up onto the bank and calmly greeted his terrified friends, who came racing down to see if he was all right.

He *was* all right. And Mustard was even *better* than all right. The quiet horse that clambered out of the river was very different from the one that had zoomed off the cliff. He didn't feel much like bucking anymore. He suddenly felt very happy to let the person in the saddle do the driving. John shook the water out of his hat, wiped his face and handed the reins to the young cowboy. Thanks to him, there would be no more trouble with *that* horse.

Please come inside John's cabin. The scent of wood is so home-like. Maybe this house does seem a little small, but John and his wife lived here pretty comfortably with their five children, managing their own ranch with 300 cattle, a couple of horses, a bunch of chickens and a dog named Bismarck. John had worked very hard for many years to make this dream come true, and this cozy cabin must have seemed like a paradise compared to the horrors of his childhood.

He'd been born on a plantation in South Carolina (some people say southern Texas). His mother and father and his ten brothers and sisters were also slaves. They were forced to work long hours in the fields, to do whatever the slave owner said, and even to fight against one another just to amuse him. Sometimes they were whipped. John's brother George lost his eye when a woman hit him with a switch, and John was once beaten with a snakeskin. For the rest of his life this big brave man was absolutely terrified of snakes.

When John was about twenty years old, slavery was finally outlawed in the United States, and the slaves were set free. He found work on a ranch near Fort Worth, Texas, and became a cowboy.

At that time almost a third of the cowboys in the American Southwest were black. Most of them were former slaves. On the ranch they often did the humblest jobs, and on cattle drives they frequently got stuck with the dirty and exhausting position of dragman at the back of the herd. John did plenty of those humble jobs, too. But he also discovered that he had a special gift — a gift that soon caught the eye of Mr. Blandon and the other cowboys at the ranch. He had an amazing ability to tame unbroken horses. He wasn't like the horse-whisperers you hear about today. He broke horses by riding them hard until they realized he was stronger and tougher than they were. Then they settled down and let him be the boss.

Let's stop for a moment so you can touch the cowboy

equipment in this display. Run your fingers over that sturdy piece of rope. Feel the smooth leather chaps and the cold branding iron. John was an expert at handling all of these tools. And yet, when he tried to join a cattle drive in 1882, the boss didn't want him.

John's friend Bill Moodie insisted. He refused to join the drive unless John was hired as well. So even though the boss only wanted Moodie, he reluctantly signed them both up. But John was assigned the worst job. He had to stay up all night and watch the herd by himself. He was given a broken saddle and a tired old horse. Maybe the boss hoped he would get mad and quit.

But he didn't. Instead, he became the most patient and reliable night-herder who ever rode the range. He joked and laughed with the other cowboys. Week after week, he did more than his share of the work. And when the right moment came he asked, "Do you think I could have a little better saddle and a little worse horse?" (He didn't really mean a *worse* horse. He meant a more spirited one, a horse with more get-up-and-go.)

"Sure," said the boss. "Here's a worse horse for you." And he pointed to a bronco that was as dangerous as a tiger, a horse so wild that no one had ever been able to sit on his back, even for an instant.

"All right," said John.

Everybody, even the cook, gathered to watch. They could hardly wait to see him get pitched through the air. They wanted to see that gangster horse dance on John's head. He eased himself into the saddle and the horse was released. The bronco exploded into the corral. It jumped, bucked and twisted like a Tasmanian Devil. It bellowed. It kicked. It pawed the air. John bellowed, too, just for show. But he stuck to that horse like chewing gum while the other cowboys stared in amazement. He was the best rider they had ever seen.

When he got off, the others rushed forward to congratulate him. He just smiled and said gently that this "worse horse" would suit him just fine. The boss was glad to have such a great rider on his team. Later John was promoted to the day crew. And by the time they reached the end of the trail, he was riding near the front of the herd on his fine spirited horse.

The journey had lasted four months. It ended near the new little town of Calgary. The province of Alberta didn't exist yet. The gorgeous, wide-open land was called The North-West Territory (which is not the same thing as our modern-day Northwest Territories) and the name of the ranch was "The North-West Cattle Company." Everyone called it "The Bar U Ranch." It was run by a man named Fred Stimson, who needed some cowboys to stay and work with the new herd.

"Who's the best?" he asked.

The trail boss answered him in a low voice. Immediately, Mr. Stimson turned to John and said, "I'll pay you $25 a month to come and work on my ranch." John said, "Not unless you hire my friend Bill Moodie, as well." So Mr. Stimson hired them both.

During his time at the Bar U Ranch, and later at a place called the Quorn Ranch, John worked hard and saved his money. First he built a cabin of spruce logs. Then he officially registered his 9999 brand, which some people called "the walking stick" brand. Then he bought nine cows. But as he worked, he was keeping another dream quietly in his heart — he wanted marriage and children.

One day he heard that a new black family had moved into the neighbourhood. He put on his best clothes and travelled 40 kilometres to visit them.

Can you guess what happened? Of course you can. He took one look at the beautiful daughter Mildred and fell in love. And naturally Mildred soon became starry-eyed, too. The whole thing was just like a chapter out of a romance novel.

One day when John and Mildred were out driving in the family's buggy, storm clouds appeared in the prairie sky. Reluctantly they turned the buggy back toward Mildred's home. But the storm overtook them. The sky turned as dark as night. Thunder crashed. Suddenly a bolt of lightning shot straight out of the sky and zapped the horses. Both of them. Dead on the road. (I am not making this up.)

John didn't hesitate. He unhitched the dead horses, picked up the buggy poles and dragged that buggy all the way home. By himself. (Honest.)

Shall we skip ahead to the wedding bells? On February 29, 1892, John and Mildred were married. And for a few years they lived happily ever after.

Happy Events in John and Mildred's Life
1892–1901

Please rank the following events in order of happiness from "not bad" to "absolutely delightful":

1. When an angry steer suddenly charged at a group of cowboys, John saved them by grabbing the animal by the horns and wrestling it to the ground.

2. At a fair in Calgary, he roped and tied a steer in 51 seconds. He was the first person to demonstrate steer wrestling in Canada. He won an expensive saddle.

3. He and Mildred had six children, including one set of twins (Nettie, Bob, Mildred, Billy, Arthur and Daniel).

4. They built a new cabin near the Red Deer River, far from busy Calgary.

5. They increased the size of their herd to 300 head of cattle.

6. Mildred taught John (who had never learned how to read or write) how to sign his own name.

Note: *Would your answer change if I told you the expensive handmade saddle was worth $100?*

For a decade or so, John and Mildred had happy adventures together. And then they didn't. It hurts me even to tell you what happened. But I must. You can't just end your essay with the words:

The rest of John Ware's life is too painful to write about.
The End.

Your teacher wouldn't like it. So please consider the following.

Sad Events in John and Mildred's Life
1901–1905

Please rank the following in order of awfulness:

1. Their youngest child, Daniel, died.

2. Their cabin was destroyed in a flood. In order to rebuild it on higher ground, he had to salvage some logs from the river and drag them to the new site.

3. Mildred accidentally walked too close while John was splitting wood, and his axe cut her head. Luckily, the wound was not too serious, and she did recover. But *OW!*

4. The cattle caught a serious disease called mange.

5. Many of their cattle died in a spring blizzard.

6. Mildred got sick and John took her to a hospital in Calgary. Ten days later she died of typhoid and pneumonia.

7. Because John couldn't work the ranch and care for the children at the same time, he sent them away to live with their grandparents in Calgary. He became very lonely.

Note: *Would your answer change if I told you an even sadder event was still to come?*

On September 1, 1905, Alberta officially became a Canadian province. Eleven days later John was out in the fields as usual, riding his grey mare, Flaxie. He was trying to separate a steer from the rest of the herd. Suddenly Flaxie tripped in a badger hole and fell on top of him. The horn of the saddle crushed his chest and killed him.

Oh, dear, I'm sorry! I shouldn't have sprung that awful event on you so suddenly. It must have given you a shock.

John's family and friends must have felt that way, too, when they got the news. One day he was alive and healthy, and the next he was gone.

At his funeral the church was packed with people — more than any other funeral since the founding of Calgary. The minister said: "John Ware was a man with a beautiful skin. Every human skin is as beautiful as the character of the person who wears it . . . He leaves me with the thought that black is a beautiful colour." People still remember John proudly. After his death, a creek, a ridge and a mountain were named after him. There's a John Ware High School, a John Ware Trail, a John Ware college building and a John Ware 4-H Beef Club.

I think he would be surprised to know that, don't you? I can almost hear him laughing his great big laugh.

FACTS FACTS FACTS FACTS

Just the Plain Facts about John Ware

1845 He was born in the southern United States, the tenth of eleven children.

1863 The Emancipation Proclamation declared that slaves must be freed.

1866 John lived in Texas and worked as a cowboy.

1882 He joined a cattle drive, taking 3000 cattle from Idaho to Calgary. When the drive was over he stayed on at the Bar U Ranch.

1884 He applied for a quarter section of land and built a cabin.

May 25, 1885
He registered Brand 9999 for his own cattle.

After September 7, 1885
He was put in charge of the horse herd at the Quorn Ranch, where horses were bred for fox hunting in England.

1888 He started his own small ranch on the north fork of Sheep Creek.

1892 He married Mildred Lewis in Calgary's Baptist Church.

1892 At a Calgary fair he roped and tied a steer in only 51 seconds.

1901 The family moved to Millarville, near present-day Brooks, where he built a log cabin on the bank of the Red Deer River.

Spring 1902
The cabin was destroyed in a flood, but he salvaged some logs and rebuilt it on higher ground.

Spring 1905
His wife died.

September 12, 1905
John was killed when his horse tripped and fell on him.

July 20, 2002
The restored cabin was unveiled in a ceremony at Dinosaur Provincial Park, near Brooks, Alberta.

LOUIS CYR AND THE BAD ADVICE

Don't be alarmed. We're a little lost, but I know we're not far from Sainte Jean de Matha, Quebec. This forest reminds me of the woods where Louis Cyr first worked as a lumberjack, cutting down great big trees and carrying them around like Popsicle sticks. (Back then, he was called Noé-Cyprien Cyr, but let's just call him Louis, so we won't get confused.)

Once, when he was twelve years old, Louis was walking through a forest just like this one. All of a sudden he heard a scary groaning sound. Luckily, it was not a ghost or a monster. It was Monsieur Gagnon, who had hurt his leg while he was chopping wood. He was sitting on a fallen log, moaning in pain, and Louis hurried to help him. But Monsieur Gagnon couldn't walk a single step, not even if he leaned hard on Louis's very strong shoulder. So he told the boy to go back to the village as fast as he could and send help.

But did Louis obey him? *Non.* He saw a much quicker and easier way to solve the problem. He picked up Monsieur Gagnon, slung him across his shoulders like a hockey bag, carried him several hundred metres through the woods and set him down gently in his wagon.

Pardon? No, Monsieur Gagnon was not a pipsqueak. He was a full-grown man who weighed about 73 kilograms, and he was absolutely astonished by the boy's strength. Why, Louis had carried him as if he weighed no more than a kit-

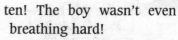

ten! The boy wasn't even breathing hard!

After he recovered from his shock, Monsieur Gagnon said *merci* for the help. Then he offered that amazing boy a job as a lumberjack's helper.

In 1875, when Louis rescued Monsieur Gagnon, his family was desperate for money. They had a lot of mouths to feed. Louis was the eldest child, and at that time he already had six younger brothers and sisters. Later, there would be seventeen children in his family. No wonder they needed his help!

Louis came from a family of strong people. He had a regular-strength father named Pierre Cyr, an extra-strength grandfather named Pierre Cyr, and a super-strength great-grandfather also named Pierre Cyr. But none of them had Louis's amazing ultra-super-extra-strength abilities. The only person who even came close in that department was his mother.

Her name was Philomène. She stood two metres tall in her stocking feet and weighed 110 kilograms. She used to sling a 100-kilo bag of flour over her shoulder and climb a ladder to put it in the attic. She could carry two full sacks of grain, one under each arm. And if her seventeen children started to act up, they soon regretted it. Once, when her grown son (named Pierre) got into a fistfight with his friend, she hoisted him off his feet, pinned him to the kitchen wall and kept him dangling there until he calmed down. Later, when her husband (named Pierre) bought a tavern, she became a bouncer. If the customers misbehaved, she picked them up and tossed them into the street.

Little Louis also spent a lot of time with his grandfather (named Pierre). He gave Louis some advice about life — some good advice, some not-so-good advice, and one piece of advice so bad it actually killed him.

Advice for Little Louis Cyr
by his Well-Meaning Grandfather (Named Pierre)

Please rank the following according to the Plumley Norris Harmfulness Scale™:

Lesson #1: The best name in the world is "Pierre."

Lesson #2: Being strong is the most important thing in the world.

Lesson #3: You should use your strength for good, not evil.

Lesson #4: If you want to get stronger, you should practise and train hard.

Lesson #5: Strong people should be gentler and kinder than other people.

Lesson #6: Strength comes from food. Eat until you're full. Then eat more and more and more and more and more and more and more and more and more.

Plumley Norris Harmfulness Scale™

1. If the thing is *useful and important*, nod your head briskly.

2. If the thing is *neutral or harmless*, hold your head perfectly still.

3. If the thing is *stupid and dangerous*, shake your head fast while silently screaming "No!" and waving your hands.

Did you guess which lesson was the most dangerous? Congratulations! I'll tell you more about that in a moment.

When Louis was fifteen, his family moved to the United States, hoping to make a better living. The supervisor of the textile mill in Lowell, Massachusetts, saw him lift a bolt of cloth that weighed 170 kilograms, and he hired him on the spot! That's when Louis changed his name from Noé-Cyprien. Even though he and his family lived in a French-Canadian neighbourhood where everyone was perfectly comfortable with the name Noé-Cyprien, the Americans had a hard time pronouncing it. Besides, his mother liked the name Louis because it had been the name of some famous French kings. So at the age of fifteen he became Louis Cyr, and that's the name we remember him by.

Here's a quick quiz for you:

Extra-Curricular Interests
of Louis Cyr:
Hobbies and Fun

Which of the following hobbies do you think young Louis did *not* enjoy? There is only one correct answer. He did *not* enjoy:

1. playing the violin

2. jumping over tables with his feet together

3. beating up people who were smaller than himself

4. square-dancing

5. letting his mother curl his long blond hair into ringlets with her curling iron.

Answer: #3. (I'm not making this up.)

ooooo

Did you guess the correct answer? Congratulations! One of the lessons Louis learned from his grandfather (named Pierre) was that strong people must never beat up weak people, and Louis never did. Whenever he could, he helped people, and he always used his strength for good, not evil. Also, Louis's mother thought it would be nice if he followed the example of Samson in the Bible, whose hair made him strong. So Louis let his long blond hair grow out, and his mother curled it into ringlets for him. People were often fooled by his round rosy cheeks and his long blond curls. They thought he looked fat and lazy. Sometimes they even made fun of him. But not for long! When Louis went into action, he was fast and powerful and extremely agile. And *strong!* Again and again, he left people speechless.

One time a farmer tried to trick him by giving him an impossible task: to load a wagon full of bricks, hitch up the horses, drive the wagon several hundred metres and unload it before the sun went down. Louis started scooping up bricks in loads that were four times as big as a normal man could carry. Then, instead of waiting around for the horses, he hitched *himself* to the wagon, dragged it to the designated spot and unloaded it. Can you imagine the look on the farmer's face? Ha ha ha. He gave Louis a good full-time job, and after that they got along just fine. In fact the farmer, Dan Bawdy, loved to watch Louis surprise other people with his strength — like the time Louis lifted a loaded wagon that was stuck in the mud. He just shoved his back under it and heave-ho, up it went, while the driver's eyes practically popped out of his head. And Mr. Bawdy was very proud when eighteen-year-old Louis competed at a September fair in Boston, where he lifted a real live Percheron horse onto his back. Louis was immediately given the title: Strongest Man in Massachusetts.

Inspiring, isn't it? And here's something that *Louis* found inspiring: a sweet little woman named Melina Comtois. He met her at the party after his horse-lifting victory. In fact, he found her so inspiring that when she moved back to Quebec he and his whole family moved back, too. Soon Louis and Melina were so inspired that they got married.

Melina was as gentle, small and mild as Louis's mother was strong, big and bold. She and Louis made a good team. When he went on tour, giving exhibitions of his great strength, she went with him and managed the money. When he bought a tavern in Montreal, she went to work behind the counter. Now and then she would call sweetly, "Louis, can you help me?" He would reach over the counter, let her sit on the palm of his hand, lift her over the counter and set her down gently on the other side without spilling a drop from her tray full of drinks. Afterward, he might lift an enormous keg of beer onto his shoulder, or jump over a table with his feet together, to impress the customers.

In those days weightlifting was not officially a sport, as it is today, but strongmen would compete in public for prizes and for the title of Strongest Man. It wasn't long before Louis traded his title as Strongest Man in Massachusetts for Strongest Man in Canada. On a muddy field in Quebec he went head-to-head (I mean, boulder-to-boulder) with the current champion, David Michaud, who had once tried to court Melina (before she met Louis, I mean). There was nothing Michaud wanted more than to beat Louis at weightlifting. He and Louis took turns lifting rocks on which someone had painted the weights: 100 pounds, 250 pounds, 400 pounds, etc. When they had both lifted the one marked 450 pounds (that is, 204 kilos), the score was tied, and Michaud was getting mad. He hadn't thought it would be this hard to win.

Angry and determined, he struggled to lift the biggest boulder of all, which was labelled with a question mark. But he couldn't budge it. He stomped away, convinced that no human would be able lift that monster rock.

Then it was Louis's turn to try. He settled his grip on the big boulder, braced his feet, and eased it out of the mud. The audience stared. He lifted it a few centimetres, and then a few more, which was more than enough to win him the championship. But he didn't stop there. He heaved that huge boulder right up to his shoulder and held it there. Then he let it crash back into the mud. *Splat!* There was no doubt in anyone's mind, not even David Michaud's — Louis Cyr was definitely the Strongest Man in Canada. After the match, when the mystery rock was heaved onto a set of scales, it turned out to weigh 480 pounds (that is, 218 kilos, or three Plumley Norrises.)

Now, please amuse yourselves with a quiz.

Let's Get Mathematical
A Plumley Norris Brain-Teaser

Using *The List Below*, please calculate the following:

1. Louis Cyr lifted 251 kilograms with one finger. How many bottles of cola is that?

2. Louis Cyr lifted 448 kilograms with one hand. How many tigers and hamsters would that be, and how would the tigers and hamsters feel about it?

3. Louis Cyr lifted 860 kilograms with two hands. How many creatures from *The List Below* would that be? Please do not divide any of the creatures into fractions.

4. Eighteen overweight men sat on a platform while Louis Cyr lifted them on his back. The total weight of the men and the platform was 1967 kilograms. (*Interesting fact:* this is thought to be the heaviest weight ever lifted by a human being.) Choose a bunch of other stuff that would add up to the same amount. Try to choose the coolest items.

The List Below

Percheron Horse	1000 kilograms
Volkswagen Beetle (no driver)	900 kilograms
Formula One Race Car (Honda EJ12) with driver	600 kilograms
Real Live Tiger	250 kilograms
Plumley Norris.	?
Golden Retriever Dog	25 kilograms
Big Bottle of Cola (2 litres)	2 kilograms
Hamster	0.1 kilogram

Bonus Question: How much does Plumley Norris weigh? (**Note:** If you go back to the last sentence before the quiz, you can figure it out.) Is Plumley Norris heavier or lighter than Louis Cyr, who weighed about 143 kilograms in 1893?

OOOOO

Louis Cyr had worked as a lumberjack, a strongman touring all around Canada and the United States, a policeman in Montreal (where he became famous for picking up the bad guys, one under each arm, and carrying them to the police station), and a tavern owner. But what he really wanted was to earn the title of Strongest Man in the World. So he cut his hair and went to Europe, to challenge the strongmen over there.

But he was just *too* strong! After a few demonstrations it was obvious that he could easily beat anyone who was foolish enough to compete with him, and of course nobody wanted to stand up in public and be humiliated. So nobody challenged him. Louis toured around giving sold-out shows, performing for royalty and having a good time, but probably wishing he hadn't been quite so dazzling during his first few performances.

One of his admirers was a rich man called the Marquis of Queensberry, who was very proud of his strong dapple-grey

horses. He suggested a contest: two horses, pulling hard in opposite directions, with Louis in the middle! If Louis succeeded in holding them still (and not getting split in half, which would be both painful and disgusting) he could keep one of the horses as a prize.

Let me cut to the chase and just say this: Louis really enjoyed driving that horse around Montreal.

When Louis finally *did* receive his big challenge, it happened back in Chicago. In a three-hour contest on April 1, 1896, he defeated the Swedish strongman August Johnson. History doesn't record whether Mr. Johnson thought the whole thing was an April Fool's joke, but as far as we know he wasn't laughing when he said, "I can defeat any man in the world; but no man can defeat this elephant." Louis didn't mind being called an elephant. He had finally achieved his lifelong goal. He was now officially The Strongest Man in the World.

But even the Strongest Man in the World can have problems, and Louis had a BIG one:

The Strongest Man in the World Takes to His Bed
A Cautionary Tale

Once upon a time there was a boy whose grandfather (named Pierre) taught him to eat and eat and eat and eat and eat. The little boy did as he was told. At every meal he ate much more than he needed or wanted, and when he grew up, he ate even more. For his breakfast he would chow down on two kilos of pork, a loaf of bread, a whole plate of potatoes and a litre of milk. Later he would have a little snack of sausages, cheese, bread, milk and tomatoes. He also loved to hang around the house doing nothing at all. If televisions had been invented back then, he would have slumped at home all day clicking channels and scarfing potato chips.

How this boy grew up to be The Strongest Man in the World is a real mystery, but for many years he thrived on this routine. Then, suddenly, he didn't. At the age of thirty-seven he got so sick that his doctor and his family were sure he would die. He was suffering from nephritis (a kidney disease), leg paralysis and heart trouble, mainly because he'd spent his whole life overeating! From then until the day he died, he wasn't allowed to eat any food at all. He could only drink milk.

For twelve whole years The Strongest Man in the World drank milk for breakfast, lunch and dinner. His appetizers, main courses and desserts were milk. His bedtime snack was milk. For every too-big meal he'd eaten in his youth, he paid with a glass of milk. He died in 1912, probably wishing he had never taken that bad advice from his grandfather (named Pierre), and maybe feeling glad that he would never have to see another glass of milk.

Well, here we are, finally, at the Musée-halte Louis Cyr behind the town hall. Please enjoy the museum exhibits — the paintings and the statues of the Strongest Man in the World. Afterward, we'll eat our sandwiches (and drink our milk) until we're happy and full — but not one bite more! Remember the moral of the Louis Cyr story: *Mooooo!*

Just the Plain Facts about Louis Cyr

October 10, 1863
Noé-Cyprien Cyr was born in St-Cyprien-de-Napierville, south of Montreal, to Pierre Cyr (a lumberjack and farmer) and Philomène Berger.

1875 He dropped out of school at the age of twelve and went to work on Irénée Gagnon's woodlot and farm.

1878 He moved with his family to a French-Canadian neighbourhood in Lowell, Massachusetts, and went to work at a textile mill. He changed his name to Louis.

1881 Louis earned the title of Strongest Man in Massachusetts by lifting a Percheron horse on his back.

1882 He married Melina Comtois in Saint-Jean-de-Matha, Quebec, and took the title of Strongest Man in Canada from David Michaud.

1883–1885
He worked as a lumberjack, a strongman and a Montreal policeman. Then he and Melina moved back to Lowell, Massachusetts, for a short time, and later returned to Quebec. They had a son who died shortly after birth and later a daughter, Emiliana.

1885–1891
Between tours and performances, Louis ran a tavern on Rue Notre-Dame in Montreal.

Autumn 1891
Louis went to Europe, hoping to win the title of Strongest Man in the World, but he was so strong that nobody would challenge him.

January 19, 1892
At the end of his twenty-three-month tour of England he performed at the Royal Aquarium Theatre in London. After two horses were hitched to his arms he held them to a standstill and kept one of them as a prize.

1894–1899
He toured with the Ringling Brothers and Barnum and Bailey circuses, and later with his own circus.

1895 On his back he lifted a platform on which eighteen large men were sitting. It weighed 4337 pounds (1967 kilos).

April 1, 1896
He competed against Swedish strongman August Johnson and officially won the title, "The Strongest Man in the World."

1900 He developed nephritis (which used to be called Bright's Disease) from eating too much, exercising too little and neglecting his health.

March 25, 1901

He accepted a challenge from strongman Edouard Beaupré and hugged Beaupré into submission.

February 26, 1906

He lifted a platform weighing 1302 kilos, which his rival Hector Décarie was unable to budge; then he announced his retirement and gave his title to Décarie.

November 10, 1912

He died one month after his forty-ninth birthday.

L.M. MONTGOMERY: SCREAM!

One, two, three . . . *screeeeam!*

We're driving toward the village of Cavendish, in the province of Prince Edward Island. The bright blue ocean stretches toward the horizon and the farms along the road are as lovely as a postcard. But brace yourselves. Here it comes: Souvenir shops! Motels! Mini-golf! Amusement parks! Pizza joints! Are you ready? *SCREEAAM!*

Help, it's not over yet! Gas stations! Billboards! Hamburger stands! Wax museums! Scream some more — really let yourself go! *SCREEEEAAM!*

Whew. We're past the worst part.

I'll just do a little deep breathing while I park the taxi in this empty lot. Please fetch the big scrapbook from the back seat. We've got a rare chance to enjoy this place before the tourists arrive, and I want to show you something special.

TAH-DAH!

Well . . . yes . . . it does look like a big rectangular hole in the ground. Actually, it's the foundation of a long-ago house. It may not seem as fun as a waterslide, as scary as a wax museum or as cheesy as a pizza, but this is where L.M. Montgomery wrote the most famous book in Canadian history: *Anne of Green Gables*.

Question A
From the list below, choose two things that helped L.M. Montgomery to survive the trouble and loneliness of her difficult life. If you don't know the answers, just guess:

1. the unspoiled beauty of nature
2. books (reading them and writing them)
3. mini-golf

Note: If you chose #3, please answer Question B (below).

Question B: Let's Try This Again.
From the list below, choose three phrases that L.M. Montgomery used when she came home to Cavendish in 1929 and saw roads being widened and billboards and tourist attractions being built. If you don't know the answers, just guess:

1. despicable
2. deplorable
3. I hate it
4. just the loveliest thing I ever saw

Note: If you chose #4, please open your notebook and write, *I will read the wonderful book* Anne of Green Gables *as soon as possible, paying special attention to Anne's love for the unspoiled beauty of Prince Edward Island.*

Many sad things happened to this famous author, so please feel free to pass around this box of tissues while I tell you about her.

When Maud* Montgomery was not yet two years old, her mother died of tuberculosis, and a few years later her father went West to seek his fortune and never came back. So Maud Montgomery's life began in sorrow, and I'm sorry to say it went downhill from there.

THE SCRAPBOOK

Let's spread the scrapbook on the grass and write in it:

Once upon a time, there was a little girl named Maud.

Little Maud came to live with her grandparents right here on this very spot where we're sitting. No, she did not live in a rectangular hole in the ground — her story is not *quite* that sad. They had a nice comfortable home. She had plenty to eat, and respectable people to look after her. What she didn't have was — well, kindness. For example, when she was nine years old she had a grey kitten called Pussy-willow that was the softest, cutest little thing ever cuddled by a lonely child. But one day it accidentally ate some poison and died. Poor Pussy-willow! Poor Maud! She was nearly sick with grief. But did her grandparents hug her and tell her how sorry they were? No. Her grandmother said, "Some day you'll really have something to cry about."

Her grandmother couldn't stand any noise or hi-jinks in

Footnote: when you write your essay about L.M. Montgomery, please do not call her Lucy, or Lucy-Maud or Maude (with an e). She hated those names.

the house, and was so unwelcoming of Maud's friends that Maud eventually stopped inviting them home. And her grandfather was even harsher than her grandmother. So Maud was often alone, and she was often lonely.

Are you ready to turn the page of the scrapbook? My, what excellent pictures you've drawn! That grey kitten looks so sad with its four little paws in the air. And who pasted this crumpled tissue here, with Sad Story written next to it? What a unique idea. (By the way, was it a fresh tissue? Ah. Good.) Now, please turn the page.

When Maud was fifteen she went to Saskatchewan to live with her father. But by then he had remarried, and Maud did not get along *at all* with her new stepmother, who was not much older than she was. So she came back home to Cavendish.

Important Question:
Did coming home solve all of Maud's problems?
Answer:
Wouldn't *that* have been nice?

Please glue the following objects onto Page Two of the scrapbook:

1. **one thin dime:** because her grandparents wouldn't give even that much toward Maud's college education. She longed for more learning, but she had to stay home and teach piano instead.

2. **the word *Charlottetown*** (torn out of a brochure): because when her father finally sent some college money, Maud was allowed to go to Charlottetown to attend Prince of Wales College, where she crammed two years of classes into one year.

3. **a glittery letter ℬ:** because after she graduated from college, Maud worked as a schoolteacher in three different villages which began with the letter ℬ — Bideford, Belmont and Bedeque. And ℬ is also for "Brrrrr!" (which describes the winter mornings when she woke up early and wrote stories and poems before she went to work).

4. **a crystal teardrop** (torn off a free sample of contact lens solution): Please write the following sad facts beside it:
   (a) In 1898 Maud's grandfather died suddenly of a heart attack. Maud moved home to Cavendish to help her grandmother.
   (b) In 1899 her true love died suddenly of influenza.
   (c) In 1900 her father died. Now she was truly an orphan.

Would you like another tissue? Please use this one for blowing your nose, but don't paste it into the scrapbook. Add one last item:

5. **an hourglass sticker:** Brace yourself. There was one thing in the whole world that made Maud glad to be alive, and it was this homestead where we're sitting. She loved every corner of it.

Can you guess what happened?

You're right. She lost the house. When her grandfather died, Maud and her grandmother were shocked to discover that he hadn't left it to them in his will. As soon as Maud's grandmother moved away or died, Maud's uncle would get the house and Maud would have to leave. Her time was running out.

What a shock! But her grandmother was too frail to care for the place by herself, so Maud stayed to help. She couldn't leave, not even for a little holiday, and sometimes — especially in the winter — she felt so trapped and lonely that she could hardly bear it. She lived like that for twelve whole years.

Let's turn the page quickly, because something interesting is about to happen. Paste these items onto Page Three: a scrap of newspaper, a sparkly ring, a sticker in the shape of the letter W, an envelope with a stamp on it, and a picture of a lady's hat.

Next to the scrap of newspaper, write:

In 1901, Maud worked for the Halifax Daily Echo.

Her job was to proofread text, answer the phone and some-times write articles about weddings and parties. Meanwhile, she kept writing her own stories and poems, which were start-ing to be published more and more often in magazines and newspapers. The newspaper job lasted eight months. Then Maud came back home to look after her grandmother.

But at home it was harder than ever to find time to write. On top of all the cooking, cleaning, snow-shovelling, baking, repairing, caring for animals, Sunday-school teaching, sewing and gardening, she helped her grandmother run the local post office. And one customer, a certain unmarried min-ister from the local church, often stayed to chat after he picked up his mail. Please glue the sparkly ring to Page Three and write:

The Reverend Ewan Macdonald.

I'll tell you about him in a minute.

In the spring of 1905 Maud agreed to write a story for a children's magazine. She went browsing through her note-books, searching for a good idea. She found one! Weeks or months earlier she had jotted down: *Elderly couple apply to orphan asylum for a boy. By mistake, a girl is sent to them.* When she stumbled across it again in her notebook, the idea seized her imagination like the spark that ignites a firecrack-er. And it was not a magazine-story firecracker, either. It was a thrilling, rainbow-sparkles, DOUBLE BOOM explosion of a *book* idea. She decided to write a book about that orphan girl, who seemed instantly alive and lovable. The girl even had a name. It was Anne. Anne with an *e*. Anne of Green Gables.

A gable is the triangle formed between the roof and the wall of a house, like this. Maud liked a white house in Cavendish, one with green gables, so she pretended that Anne lived there. Nowadays, tourists flock to see Green Gables House, but it is just a replica of the place where Anne *might* have lived. Actually, Maud wrote most of the book right here, sitting near her own bedroom window or in the kitchen. Sometimes she perched on top of the kitchen table to catch the last of the day's sunlight.

She began writing on a rainy evening in May of 1905 and finished the book the following winter. She typed the manuscript on a clunky old typewriter that wasn't very good at making upper-case letters and wouldn't type *w* at all! (Please stick the glittery W, and the envelope with the stamp on it, into our scrapbook.) Then she mailed her story away to a publisher. First she mailed it to a small publishing company. But the editor didn't want it. Then she mailed it to a big company. That editor didn't want it, either. Then she mailed it to a few middle-sized companies, and *they* didn't want it either! Poor Maud.

After the fifth rejection she decided the book wasn't as good as she'd thought. She stuffed the manuscript in an old hatbox, stuck it in a cupboard and closed the door. (Please stick the picture of the *hat* into the scrapbook and draw a box around it.)

Maud tried to forget about the book. She went back to writing stories and poems for magazines and newspapers, and to her duties around the house and the post office. She figured that someday she would chop a lot of scenes out of

the Anne book and turn it into a magazine story that might earn thirty-five or forty dollars.

Months went by. One day when she was cleaning out the cupboard she opened the hatbox and read a few pages. The story didn't seem so bad. Maybe it wouldn't hurt to send it to one more publisher.

She mailed it to a company called L.C. Page. (*Page* was the family name of the man who owned the company, but it's a very good name for a book publisher, isn't it?) Then she got busy with other things, like her secret engagement to the minister Ewan Macdonald. Maud refused to get married as long as her grandmother still needed her. But Ewan agreed to wait. Here's a **GOLD MEDAL** that I peeled off a package of coffee. Paste it onto Page Three and write:

The Ewan Macdonald Award for Patience.

Here comes the most exciting part. Hang onto your hats! Quick, turn the page and write in big letters:

YAHOOOOO!

On April 15, 1907, Maud Montgomery received a letter from the Page Company, offering to publish *Anne of Green Gables* as a book. It was the most thrilling moment of her whole life! And along with the thrill came another thing: Money.

Maud's Money
A Difficult Choice

The Page Company offered Maud a choice. Which would *you* choose?

Would you rather have $500 total (which was about twice as much as you could earn for one year of teaching) **OR** 9¢ every time a copy of your book was sold?

Maud thought about it. She did a little math. She decided to trust that the book would sell at least 5555 copies, and she chose Offer #2. Please write again:

YAHOOOOO!

Anne of Green Gables was published in June of 1908 and — **POW!** — like an exploding firecracker, it became an instant success. People *loved* it. Within six months it was on the bestseller charts in ten cities. Nine cents per book really added up and Maud's first royalty cheque was $1730! By the end of 1910 she had earned $7000. It would have taken *twenty-five years* of teaching to earn that much money.

THE PAGE COMPANY JUNE 1908
PAY TO THE ORDER OF L.M. MONTGOMERY $1,730.00
ONE THOUSAND SEVEN HUNDRED & THIRTY XX/DOLLARS
L.C. Page

Important Question:

Did riches and success solve all of Maud's problems?

Answer:

Wouldn't *that* have been nice?

Maud was still determined to look after her grandmother as long as necessary and to prevent Uncle John from taking over the homestead, but oh my, it was difficult work. Even though Maud was thirty-four years old and a successful author, her grandmother still wouldn't allow her to:

(1) make any changes or improvements to the house

(2) go to bed later than 9:00 p.m.

(3) light a fire in any stove or fireplace except in the kitchen, even if Maud was shivering

(4) take a bath more often than once every two weeks

(5) sweep her bedroom too often

(6) bake a new cake if there was even one dried-up old slice still left in the pantry

(7) cry

Please write:

Money isn't everything.

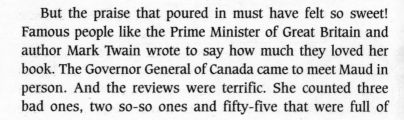

But the praise that poured in must have felt so sweet! Famous people like the Prime Minister of Great Britain and author Mark Twain wrote to say how much they loved her book. The Governor General of Canada came to meet Maud in person. And the reviews were terrific. She counted three bad ones, two so-so ones and fifty-five that were full of compliments far beyond her highest hopes.

Two buses have just turned into the parking lot, and here come some tourists with their cameras and guidebooks. Let's walk down to Cavendish Beach while I tell you what happened next. As we cross the highway and make our way toward the beach, please try not to be distracted by the tourist shops and amusements. Try to see this shoreline as it would have been when Maud lived here — the silky dunes and rugged red cliffs plunging down toward the ocean. Isn't it spectacular?

In 1911 Maud Montgomery's whole life changed, as she had always known it would. In March her grandmother caught pneumonia and died. Even though they hadn't always gotten along, it was still a terrible shock. She'd been like a mother to Maud.

Four months after her grandmother died, Maud and Ewan got married. Sit here on this sun-warmed dune, spread out the scrapbook and listen to the cries of the seagulls.

Here's an unhappy truth: Maud didn't really love Ewan. She *liked* him. And he had waited five whole years for her to be free. And she wanted to live in a nice house with a nice respectable husband and — she hoped — have some children. But Ewan was not exactly the man of her dreams, not a *kindred spirit*, as Anne would say. And Maud knew that. But she married him anyway.

I won't say that *every* sorrow that followed was because of that big decision. But many sorrows did come after that wedding day. Maud moved with Ewan to Ontario, and she never lived on her beloved Island again. One of her babies was stillborn. Another son got into a lot of trouble — that broke her heart. She spent years in court fighting the Page

Company, which had published one of her manuscripts without permission, and even though she won the lawsuits she lost all her money in the Great Depression. Her best friend suddenly died. Uncle John tore down the house. Ewan became mentally ill, and Maud spent years covering up for him so he wouldn't lose his job. The strain was so terrible that her own health began to fail. She had to have all her teeth pulled out. She suffered from anxiety and depression. She fell and hurt herself and . . . well, all right. I'll go straight to the very sad ending of her story. On April 24, 1942, she died in Toronto. Ewan brought her coffin back to Cavendish, and she is buried in a cemetery just up the hill from here.

Oh, dear. What a lot of sad things are recorded here on Page Five! Let's turn the page and cheer ourselves up. For example, you can record the fact that — in spite of her troubles — Maud Montgomery published 24 books (8 were about Anne), 230 stories and more than 500 poems, and her writing was full of love and laughter. Also, she adored nature. A glimpse of pine trees against the sky or a solitary walk along the beach — these things could made her feel glad to be alive.

What a beautiful scrapbook you've made! When you go back to the classroom it will remind you of this lovely day. Good work!

Splat!

Oh NO! Did you see that? A seagull flew over and . . . oh, *dear* . . . what a mess it made, right on Page Six! Ugh. I'll clean it up with a tissue while you run down to the beach. You can hunt for seashells, just as Maud did when she was your age. Dance and jump until you feel glad to be alive. And while you're at it — don't forget to *SCREEEEEAM!*

Just the Plain Facts about L.M. Montgomery

November 30, 1874
> She was born in Clifton (now called New London) on Prince Edward Island, to Hugh Montgomery and Clara Woolner Macneill.

1876 Her mother died of tuberculosis, and a few years later her father moved to Saskatchewan, so she was raised by her grandparents, Lucy Woolner and Alexander Marquis Macneill.

1890 She travelled to Saskatchewan to stay with her father. Her poem about a P.E.I. legend was published in the Charlottetown *Daily Patriot*.

August 1891
> She returned to her grandparents' home in Cavendish, P.E.I.

September 1893
> She attended Prince of Wales College in Charlottetown.

1894 She taught school in Bideford, P.E.I.

1895 She studied English literature at Dalhousie University.

1896–1897
She taught school in Belmont, P.E.I.

March 5, 1898
Her grandfather died of a heart attack and she returned to Cavendish to live with her grandmother.

January 16, 1900
Her father died.

Autumn 1901
She worked for the *Daily Echo* newspaper in Halifax, but returned to Cavendish after eight months to live with her grandmother.

Spring 1905
She began writing *Anne of Green Gables.*

January 1906
She sent "Anne" to several publishers, one after another.

April 15, 1907
Anne of Green Gables was accepted for publication.

June 20, 1908
She received her first copy of the book.

March 1909
She finished writing a sequel (*Anne of Avonlea*).

March 5, 1911
Her grandmother died of pneumonia.

July 5, 1911
She married Ewan Macdonald and they moved to Leaskdale, Ontario. Between 1912 and 1915 she bore three sons, but one did not live.

1916 She entered into two lawsuits against her publisher.

January 1919
Her best friend (and cousin) Frederica Campbell died.

Early 1920
Her husband started showing signs of mental/
emotional illness; she hid the fact from everyone
for fear he would lose his job.

January 1923
She was the first Canadian woman to be named a
Fellow of the Royal Society of Arts in England.

1926 She and her family moved to Norval, Ontario.

October 1929
She lost much of her money in the famous stock
market crash.

1935 She and Ewan retired and moved to a house called
Journey's End in Toronto. She was elected to the
Literary and Artistic Institute of France, and became
an Officer of the Order of the British Empire.

1940 She injured herself in a fall.

April 24, 1942
She died in Toronto and was buried in Cavendish, P.E.I.

1965 The musical version of *Anne of Green Gables* was first
presented in Charlottetown and is still an annual
event

The Anne Books: *Anne of Green Gables, Anne of Avonlea, Anne of the
Island, Anne of Windy Poplars, Anne's House of Dreams, Anne of Ingleside,
Rainbow Valley* and *Rilla of Ingleside*
The Emily Books: *Emily of New Moon, Emily Climbs* and *Emily's Quest*
The Pat Books: *Pat of Silver Bush* and *Mistress Pat*

BILLY BISHOP AND THE LUCK OF THE DEVIL

Hold on tight! As we drive through the meadow, our big black taxi is going to bounce like crazy. Whoah! This — must — be — how — Billy — Bishop — felt — when his — airplane — was — bumping — across — the — field — at — Filescamp — Farm! Maybe — his — teeth — rattled — and — his — bones — got — shaken — up — just — like — this! Hang — on — just — a — few — more — seconds. Whew. I'll park here beside the barn.

Please help me lift the radio-controlled model plane out of the trunk. Isn't it a beauty? It's an exact replica of the Nieuport Scout flown by Billy Bishop during World War I. Pretend we're in France. Yes, it would have been nice to go there in person, but we don't have enough money or time to fly all the way across the ocean, so we're here at my friend's farm in Quebec.

In March, 1917, a young pilot named Billy Bishop arrived here — I mean, at an aerodrome* called Filescamp Farm, in France — ready and eager to fight the Germans. But his flying career almost ended before it started.

Footnote: aerodrome: AIR-o-drome. *n.* a landing field for aircraft; an airport.

It wasn't like Billy to have such bad luck. His friends said he had "the luck of the devil." For example:

Nugget-O'-Luck #1 ♣

Billy Arrives Alive

Billy Bishop was on his way to Europe to fight in World War I. After a fourteen-day trip across the North Atlantic, the convoy of ships in which he was travelling neared the coast of Ireland. Suddenly the convoy was attacked by German submarines. While Billy watched, three of the other ships sank and 300 soldiers were killed. But Billy's ship, *The Caledonia*, arrived safely in England without a scratch.

Billy soon discovered that he hated the mud and struggle that went with being in the infantry, so he became a pilot instead. But takeoffs and landings were never his best subject, and shortly after he got to Filescamp Farm he made a landing that was less than perfect. Actually, it was a crash. Billy wasn't hurt (Lucky!) but his plane buried its nose in the mud and lay there, waiting for first aid. Still worse, an important general happened to be visiting that day. He hauled Billy aside and ordered him straight back to flight school. (Unlucky!) But while Billy was waiting for transportation back to flight school, some German planes attacked. (Only Billy Bishop could make something lucky out of *that!*)

The English pilots, including Billy, ran to their machines and scrambled into the cockpits. The engines roared. The ground crews yanked the blocks away from the wheels and the airplanes trundled across the field. One by one they took off and assumed their positions in the air like big noisy dragonflies. As a rookie, Billy brought up the rear.

Nobody expected a rookie pilot to do more than stay alive in an air battle — especially a rookie who had been ordered back to flight school because of his bad landings. But Billy surprised everyone. He was quick. He was gutsy. He could shoot like a veteran. He flew straight at a German plane and shot it down, chasing it through a steep dive that strained his newly mended airplane to the limit. His engine stalled and he was forced to land very close to the front lines, where shells were crashing and exploding all around. A day and a half later, when he finally arrived back at Filescamp Farm in a truck, towing his Nieuport, everyone was so impressed that they treated him like a hero. And they decided he didn't have to go back to flight school after all. Lucky!

Billy's second month with the squadron became known as Bloody April. The average life expectancy of a rookie pilot was just three weeks, and during a certain three-day period, ten of the eighteen pilots in Billy's squadron died. But Billy thrived. He flew three, four or five missions a day — many more than he was required to. And he flew them solo.

In those days you had to be lucky just to survive the flying. There wasn't even a roof over the pilot's head. He wore a leather helmet to keep his ears from freezing.

Nugget-O'-Luck #2 ♣
Billy's Helmet Saves His Life

Early in his flying career, Billy was an observer, taking reconnaissance photos while somebody else did the flying. One day, while he was doing this, something appeared out of thin air and whacked the side of his leather helmet, bruising his head. Billy was astonished. It was anti-aircraft fire, blasting out of guns on the ground, and it almost never hit the planes or pilots. He wasn't seriously hurt, but he was incredibly lucky — had he been hit a few centimetres to the left or right, it would almost certainly have ended his life.

Nugget-O'-Luck #3 ♣
Billy's Helmet Nearly Kills Him

Billy's wife once sent him an expensive new helmet lined with zebra fur. She chose the largest size because his head was unusually big, and the helmet fit quite loosely. One day, just as four German planes were diving to attack him, Billy's new helmet slid around and completely covered his face. He couldn't see a thing! He heard the Germans open fire as he clawed at the helmet and finally managed to push it out of the way. As he regained his vision he expected to see the enemy closing around him. But to his amazement, they had zoomed past and were now safely out of range far below. (History does not record whether they missed him because they were laughing so hard.)

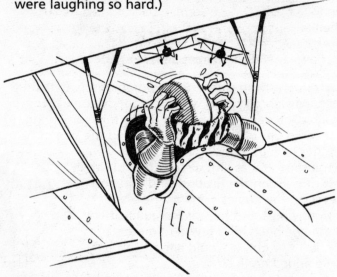

Most pilots also wore goggles, but Billy never did. He didn't want anything to interfere with his incredible vision — he could see enemy aircraft across amazing distances. He steered with his whole body — both hands on the throttle and his feet on the wooden pole that controlled the rudder — leaning right or left to turn the plane, holding the throttle between his knees when he had to change his machine gun ammunition drum. In those early days, flying was more like skiing than driving. And if that wasn't scary enough, the pilots were always in danger of being shot, or crashing, or catching on fire. It took incredible courage just to go up in the air.

Nugget-O'-Luck #4 ♣

Billy Shoots Down his First Enemy Aircraft

On March 25, 1916, a German pilot named Renatus Theiller shot down his first airplane. Exactly one year later, on March 25, 1917, Billy Bishop shot down his first airplane, firing his machine gun into the cockpit and watching the bullets strike the seat and the pilot. Seconds later the German plane crashed to the ground, killing Renatus Theiller. Lucky for Billy. Not lucky for Renatus.

Nugget-O'-Luck #5 ♣

Billy's Lucky Thirteen

Around noon on April 23, 1917, a German pilot named Paul von Osterroht destroyed a British airplane and counted it as his seventh victory. About six hours later he was shot out of the sky. Billy Bishop's "lucky thirteenth" victory was not so lucky for Paul von Osterroht, who was killed in action.

Off duty, Billy and the other members of 60 Squadron played with the farmer's rabbits and teased his ducks. They adopted stray dogs — including a smelly one that was Billy's special favourite — and they painted the farmer's pigs in patriotic colours.

Billy was full of zany ideas, like pouring champagne into the piano, sneaking up on a friend and ripping the uniform off his back, or setting the barracks on fire. If *you* did any of those things you'd be grounded for a *month*, or even arrested. But Billy's commanding officers didn't punish him. His crazy pranks helped to distract the other pilots from the fact that they were likely to die very soon and very violently. They desperately needed his jokes and his courage.

Some of Billy's squadron-mates agonized before a mission. Some of them got sick, broke down or had nightmares. Most were so exhausted when they returned after a patrol that the last thing they wanted was to go up again. But Billy would gobble some lunch and take off again by himself, flying deep into enemy territory, hunting for Germans. And even he had some close calls that would haunt him for the rest of his life.

Nugget-O'-Luck #6 ☘

Billy's Close Call

On July 28, 1917, Billy's worst fear came true when enemy bullets smashed into his airplane and set it on fire. With smoke and flame pouring from his machine, he struggled to land. A tree loomed up and he crashed into it. He ended up stuck in the plane, upside-down, in his burning Nieuport. Luckily, a sudden downpour came along and doused the fire. Also luckily, there happened to be a couple of friendly soldiers nearby, who rushed over and pulled him from the plane. Luckily, Billy was not physically hurt in the crash, but he did have nightmares about it for many years afterward, complete with realistic sound effects of crackling flames and raindrops.

During World War I, a pilot who destroyed at least five enemy planes was called an ace, and Billy Bishop was an ace among aces. He shot down so many enemy planes that the nose of his Nieuport Scout was painted blue to show that he was a top scorer. When his friends were killed, he turned his grief into hatred against the enemy and fought harder than ever, earning medal after medal for his courage.

One time he risked his life in a wildly dangerous attack on an observation balloon, chasing it down to the ground, shooting the crew, and driving down an enemy airplane in the process. For "conspicuous gallantry and devotion to duty" he received the Military Cross.

Another time he zoomed into a group of three enemy airplanes and managed to shoot down two of them, even though he was under attack from other enemy planes at the same time. He was awarded the Distinguished Service Order.

But his biggest award, and his most famous achievement, was the Victoria Cross. He received that for his brave and amazing solo attack on a German aerodrome.

It's impossible to talk about Billy Bishop's Victoria Cross without mentioning **The Big Controversy**. This is annoying, but it can't be helped. Sorry.

The Big Controversy
According to Plumley Norris

Sixty or seventy years after Billy Bishop won the Victoria Cross, someone started asking questions about whether his famous aerodrome attack really happened. All of the evidence which could prove it — or disprove it — disappeared a long time ago, but that didn't stop historians from arguing, and they're still at it. They bicker. They squabble. They say things like, "he would have," "he couldn't have" and "he must have." I can't solve the aerodrome mystery for you. Nobody can. So when you're writing your essay about Billy Bishop, please don't take my word for what happened. Read about the controversy. Make up your own mind. State your opinion boldly. Here's the Plumley Norris version:

Billy Bishop's Aerodrome Raid
June 2, 1917

At 3:00 a.m. Billy Bishop crawled out of his bunk and tried one last time to get his friend Willy Fry to fly with him on a daring raid across enemy lines. Willy said *"No!"* and went back to sleep.

At 3:57 a.m. Billy took off alone into a light drizzle. He flew straight into enemy territory. He thought he could find an aerodrome at a place called Estourmel and attack the planes while they were still on the ground, when the enemy wasn't expecting it. But when he got to Estourmel there wasn't a single German plane in sight.

Billy flew southeast for 6 or 7 kilometres. Finally, near a village called Esnes, he saw four sheds, an airplane hangar and some vehicles parked on the road, plus seven German airplanes — six scout planes and a "two-seater." This was a lucky break for Billy, but not for the German unit, which was on its way to Flanders to prepare for a British attack. The aerodrome that Billy had stumbled across was temporary. The sheds and hangar were here today, gone tomorrow — now you see it, now you don't. Or, in Billy's case, now you see it, now you shoot.

The German planes were idling their engines. Billy flew straight at them, firing his machine gun. When the first plane took off he fired thirty rounds of ammunition into it and watched it crash. Ditto the second German plane. Meanwhile, two more planes had taken off. He zoomed toward one of them, still firing, and watched it crash on the ground. The second of the pair began to chase him, and he fired a whole drum of ammunition at it until it finally stopped its attack.

As he headed for home Billy suddenly saw four more enemy planes above him. He flew along below them on a heading that made it hard for them to spot him. Then he broke off to the west and made a clean getaway without being seen. Lucky! But he wasn't safe yet.

As he flew along he began to feel very strange — dizzy, sick to his stomach and afraid of fainting. To make matters worse, he was lost. So he landed in a farmer's field to ask, "Which way to the front?" The farmer got him pointed in the right direction and Billy arrived back at Filescamp Farm at 5:40 a.m., firing off his flare gun as he always did to let his fellow pilots know that his attack had been successful. When he climbed out of the cockpit, everyone gathered round to marvel at what he had done. They found bullet holes in the tail of his plane and along one of the lower wings where the edge had been shot away.

His commanding officer, Jack Scott, was thrilled with Billy's daring exploit, and recommended him for the Victoria Cross — the highest award for gallantry in the whole British Empire!

Oh, dear. It's starting to rain now. Grab the model plane

and hurry into the barn. It's dim and chilly, but pretend we're in the throne room of Buckingham Palace. Those surprised-looking chickens are famous generals and politicians, waiting for the awards ceremony to begin. But Billy Bishop is *late*!

This is not his fault. No one has ever received *three* decorations (that's what the British military call medals) at the same time, so the officials haven't been sure what to do with him. Behind the scenes, they've hurried him from one room to another. Now that they've finally got him sorted out, there's no time to rehearse. He's standing there in the doorway of the stall — I mean the hall — while the King and all the important chickens — I mean guests — sit looking at him. He's terrified! But he takes a deep breath and marches forward.

Oh no! He can't believe his ears! His boot is squeaking! One step — *squeeek!* Two steps — *squeeek!* Three . . . He takes ten noisy paces. It feels like a hundred. In the middle of this big room he turns and bows to the guests. When he stands at attention before King George V, his face is red and he is quaking with nerves. The King makes him wait while a servant carries the decorations around the room on a satin cushion, showing them off to the guests. Then an officer begins to talk about each one: the Military Cross, the Distinguished Service Award and the Victoria Cross. After the King gets all three lined up nicely on Billy's chest he stands and chats with him for several minutes, which for Billy is more agonizing than a dogfight. Later, he'll tell his fiancée it was too awful for words. But finally he's allowed to escape . . . *Squeeek, squeeeek, squeeeek* . . .

Afterward, important people in London began inviting him to social events — a whirlwind of congratulations and celebrations — but finally he went back to the front, where he shot down more enemy planes than ever and became more and more famous every day.

Nugget-O'-Luck #7 ♣

Billy's Helmet Saves his Life (Again)

German bombers arrived near Dunkirk and the air raid sirens sounded. As Billy walked toward a dugout, a sergeant stopped him and told him to put on a steel helmet. Billy confessed he'd forgotten his, and to make a point, the sergeant handed over his own. Annoyed, Billy shoved it on his head. Seconds later a powerful blow sent him reeling. A piece of flying shrapnel had crashed into the helmet, denting it and wrenching his neck. Without it, the blow would have split his skull wide open. Billy was lucky!

The more famous Billy became, the more the Canadian government pressured him to retire. They didn't want to take the chance that their most famous ace would get killed. Billy Bishop was now more valuable as a celebrity than he was in the cockpit. So at last the order came down. His last day at the front would be June 19, 1918.

Billy was like a desperate football player in the final minutes of a game, trying to score one touchdown after another. In his last three days, he flew constantly. In his last *twelve minutes*, he brought down five enemy aircraft. That's more than most pilots brought down during the entire war. When it was all over, his score stood at 72. Only two other pilots shot down more planes than he did. One was Frenchman René Fonck (who shot down 75 enemy aircraft and never got especially famous). The other was a German pilot named Manfred von Richthofen — the Red Baron — who shot down 80 planes and became very famous.

Canadians welcomed Billy home as their first-ever international hero, and for months he was mobbed by cheering crowds wherever he went. He was the most highly decorated fighter alive — altogether, he'd earned ten decorations. He wrote a book about his experiences and travelled around giving lectures. When World War II broke out he became Honorary Air Marshal of the Royal Canadian Air Force, which was the highest rank in the Canadian forces.

The rain is stopping now, and that rainbow over the cedar trees looks very lucky, doesn't it? Let's put the Nieuport Scout down on the grass. If you ignore that chicken and squint your eyes just so, it looks exactly like a real plane, just waiting for Billy to climb into the cockpit.

Just the Plain Facts about Billy Bishop

February 8, 1894

William Avery Bishop was born in Owen Sound, Ontario, to Will Bishop and Margaret Louise Green.

Autumn 1911

He entered the Royal Military College in Kingston, Ontario.

1914 When World War I broke out, he enlisted in a Toronto cavalry unit, and later joined the 7th Canadian Mounted Rifles.

June 1915

He sailed for Europe and was posted to England, but resolved to become a pilot.

September 1915

He joined the Royal Flying Corps and flew missions as an observer.

March 1917

He reported to Fighter Squadron Number 60 at Filescamp Farm near Izel les Hameaux, France.

March 25, 1917

He participated in his first real dogfight; his engine stalled but he glided to safety near the front.

April 7, 1917

He destroyed an enemy observation balloon in an attack that earned him the Military Cross.

May 2, 1917

He participated in nine aerial fights, one of which earned him the Distinguished Service Order.

June 2, 1917

He attacked a German aerodrome by himself and earned the Victoria Cross.

August 30, 1917

He received three decorations from King George V at Buckingham Palace.

October 17, 1917

In Toronto he married Margaret Burden, the granddaughter of Timothy Eaton.

May 1918

He returned to France as the commander of a hand-picked team of pilots called 85 Squadron.

June 1918

The Canadian government asked him to return to England. During his last three days at the front he scored ten victories over enemy aircraft.

November 11, 1918

The war ended.

1920 He started a passenger air service in Toronto with friend and fellow war ace William Barker.

1939 When World War II broke out he was appointed Honorary Air Marshal of the RCAF and acted as the Director of Recruiting, travelling and lecturing extensively.

1952 He retired and moved to Palm Beach, Florida.

September 10, 1956
He died in his sleep in Palm Beach and was buried at the Greenwood Cemetery in Owen Sound.

1987 His family home in Owen Sound became the Billy Bishop Museum; on May 10, 2002, it was declared a National Historic Site.

FREDERICK BANTING DOES HIS BEST

I hope you won't mind sharing a seat with Walter. I'm looking after him for a friend. He's a Newfoundland dog the size of a refrigerator and he has a big pink tongue. (Walter, I mean. Not my friend.) You may use that towel to wipe off the drool as I back this taxi out of its parking space.

Once upon a time there was a young doctor named Fred Banting, who also knew a little something about going backward. He used to visit his parents' farm in an old Model T Ford that could only climb the steep hills in reverse, with its motor straining and groaning.

May I tell you his story backward? First I'll tell you about his death. Then I'll tell you about his career and his amazing discovery. And I'll finish up with an interesting story about his childhood. Welcome to this *Plumley Norris Field Trip and Historical Excursion (Backward Edition)*™.

Here in Gander, Newfoundland, we're heading for the North Atlantic Aviation Museum. Snow is falling thick and fast. I'll drive carefully while you consider the following:

Question #5

Would you rather:

(a) climb into a noisy old-fashioned airplane in the dark and fly across the ocean into a war zone (in the snow)?

(b) stay at home in your nice safe lab and invent things?
Fred's Answer:
"I'll do my duty, even if it kills me." And it did.

Oooh! It's shocking to begin a chapter with a dead Fred! Let's get his tragic end out of the way quickly, so we can get to the part where he saved millions of lives and grew up and was born.

Fred would have preferred to stay at home doing experiments in his lab. But in February of 1941 World War II was raging in Europe, and when he got a chance to fly to England to share his ideas with doctors who were close to the action, he agreed to go, even though the trip was so dangerous.

In those days, almost everything that crossed the Atlantic Ocean — including warplanes — was sent by ship. But by November of 1940 there was such an urgent need for planes that the Canadian military started flying them over instead. Those aircraft that actually survived the trip reached Europe much faster than they would have by sea. But the journey was risky and difficult! By the time Fred arrived in Gander, a blizzard was blowing, five planes were already stranded on the field, and everyone was feeling uneasy.

If you look out the window, you'll see what he saw: snow, snow, snow. (*I* can barely see the road.)

While Fred was stranded, a young radio operator named Tripp took him to meet some of the local military officers. When Fred was introduced, the whole company instantly snapped to attention, and Tripp just stood there staring in astonishment. He had accidentally made friends with the world famous Sir Frederick Banting, the man who had dis-

covered insulin, the first Canadian ever to win the Nobel Prize, and the first to be knighted for a scientific achievement. But Fred didn't act like a star. He sat around drinking coffee with the kitchen staff, worrying about how to use the bathroom during his long flight.

On the flight to Gander, the pilot had had to adjust the plane's balance every time Fred walked to the toilet in the tail of the plane. How embarrassing! And now Fred was facing an even longer flight!

He was stranded at Gander Airport for three days. Finally, around 8:00 p.m. on Thursday, February 20, the weather cleared. He climbed into the cold metal cabin of the plane. So Fred wouldn't have to use the plane's bathroom, Tripp gave him a package of special disposable cups as a goodbye gift.

There were only four people aboard: Fred, the pilot (Captain Mackey), a navigator and a radio operator. The noisy bomber taxied along the runway and lifted off into the night sky. Twenty minutes later, in the blackness over the ocean, one of the engines failed. Captain Mackey turned the plane around and struggled back toward the airport. He might have succeeded. But then the other engine failed.

Let's not dwell on the bone-breaking impact, or the fact

that the crash happened so deep in the woods that it took three days for rescuers to get there. Let's just say that Captain Mackey was knocked unconscious. When he woke up, the navigator and radio operator were dead and Fred was dying of a brain injury and a punctured lung. For a few hours Fred's speech was garbled and he dictated technical notes in a confused way. Captain Mackey left briefly to search for help, and when he came back — please brace yourself, this is horrible — he found Fred lying face down in the snow, dead.

Some hunters heard about the crash and hurried to the scene. They rescued Captain Mackey and used sleds to haul the bodies of the dead men to the nearby village of Musgrave Harbour. Frederick Banting's body was flown to Toronto for a big funeral and he was buried there, in Mount Pleasant Cemetery.

The End.

(Remember, we're telling this story backward, so The End actually means The Beginning. Please stay tuned.)

Meanwhile, Walter's doggy breath is steaming up the windows, and now we're trapped behind a snowplow. While we creep along, here's another question:

Question #4

Would you rather:

(a) make an amazing discovery and spend the rest of your life struggling to make another one?

(b) make an amazing discovery and spend the rest of your life going to parties, hanging out with your friends and never doing another speck of work?

Fred's Answer:
"Point me toward the lab. I've got work to do."

When Fred discovered insulin, right at the beginning of his career, it was one of the biggest medical breakthroughs ever made. Almost overnight he became world famous, and many people thought he was a genius. After his success with insulin he tried to find cures for drowning, cancer and a lung disease called silicosis. But most of his experiments failed — partly because Fred was not the greatest researcher who ever wore a lab coat.

OOPS!
Small But Silly Mistakes
Made by Frederick Banting

Please rank the following mistakes from "could have happened to anybody" to "completely silly," and imagine what your science teacher would say if *you* did them:

1. wrote sloppy and incomplete lab notes

2. accidentally switched Sample A with Sample B, and got the results backward

3. accidentally injected sugar water into a dog's lung instead of its stomach

4. forgot to take the patients' temperatures

5. killed a dog by giving it too much anaesthetic

Bonus Mistake: Please compare these little errors to the Giant Oops made by Fred's colleague, Dr. Collip, who created the first successful batch of insulin in the history of the world . . . and then *forgot* the formula!

OOPS!

Still, Fred never stopped trying to make more discoveries. For twenty years he worked hard at the University of Toronto in the big lab which had his name on it: The Banting Institute. But nothing ever came close to the thrill of those first insulin trials, so let's zoom backward in time to a certain day when he was thirty years old.

On January 23, 1922, a dying boy named Leonard Thompson received the first effective shot of insulin ever given to a diabetic person. He was fourteen years old. In those days, near starvation was the only known way to extend the life of a person with diabetes, and Leonard had been starving for months. During those months Fred and his assistant had been struggling to purify a substance they called insulin. They were pretty sure it helped to extend the lives of dogs. But would it work on *humans?*

By the time they were ready to try it, Leonard weighed just 30 kilograms, and he was as bony as a skeleton. Because of his diabetes his body couldn't convert food into usable energy, and he was almost in a coma. A previous shot of insulin had given him nothing but a pain in the backside — literally. The insulin didn't work, and to make matters worse, he developed a painful abscess at the injection site.

But the doctors tried again, using a purified type of insulin. Nobody was sure it would work, but they had nothing to lose, because without it Leonard was sure to die.

What a thrill it must have been to see that sick boy get well so suddenly! He woke up, began to move around and said he felt stronger. His diabetic symptoms went away. His blood sugar dropped to normal. The doctors were astonished — and ecstatic. Around the world, thirty million people were dying of diabetes. If insulin could help Leonard Thompson, could it help the others as well?

It could. It did. It still does.

Leonard led the way. When he started receiving insulin injections every day he regained his normal weight and began to live a healthy and active life. He lived for thirteen more years — and he might have lived even longer but, sadly, he died in a motorcycle crash.

Question #3

Would you rather:
(a) get an injection of insulin every single day of your life?
(b) starve to death slowly?
Leonard Thompson's Answer:
"Please jab me with that needle!"

Fred loved dogs. When he was growing up, he had a dog named Collie who lived in a cozy doghouse with a furry rug and a nice little porch. And when Fred began to experiment with insulin, he couldn't help loving some of the dogs that were his test subjects. When they died, he sometimes cried. But he never gave up on his research.

The traffic is finally moving again. Would you please cover Walter's ears? I don't want him to hear this part: Fred made those dogs diabetic on purpose. He took out their pancreases. Then he tried to make them well again with extracts made from the pancreases of other dogs and from the pancreases of unborn cows. He began his experiment with ten dogs, but — are you sure Walter's ears are covered? — before long, every single dog had died of diabetes, shock or infection. So Fred and his partner, Charley Best, climbed into Fred's Model T Ford and went dog hunting. They offered a dollar to anybody who could bring them a stray dog, and they managed to build up a new supply. Once, when Fred didn't have a leash, he towed an unsuspecting dog back to the lab with his tie.

You can let go of Walter's ears now. Let's flip the calendar back to the summer of 1921. Young Fred and his assistant Charley are hard at work in their hot, dusty lab. Fred can't stand the sweltering heat, so he has cut the sleeves out of his lab coat. He and Charley are rookies. They make a lot of mistakes. A lot of you-know-whats die. Fred and Charley's supervisor, Dr. Macleod, isn't very confident about their research. But Fred's idea is so exciting that it keeps them going.

Maybe you've noticed that when people get excited, especially when something important is at stake, they sometimes grow tense and fierce with one another. As Fred and Charley

began to show how insulin could make the you-know-whats live longer, Dr. Macleod and Dr. Collip jumped in to help. Soon the four men were quarrelling bitterly about the experiments. Dr. Collip purified the insulin extract and made it work. But then he refused to tell Fred how he did it. Then he *forgot* how he did it. (I'm not making this up.) One day Fred met him in the corridor, grabbed him by the collar and threatened to kick his rear-end all the way to College Street if he didn't cough up the formula. Bystanders had to pry the two men apart. Eventually (*not* because of this incident, which achieved nothing but bad feelings) Dr. Collip did re-create the formula, and the insulin testing continued.

But Fred Banting also had a kind, generous side.

Fred's Kind and Generous Side: A Few Examples

A Plumley Norris Checklist

✓ He gave half of his Nobel Prize money to Charley Best.

✓ He donated the other half of the money to the lab where the insulin was being manufactured, so patients could receive insulin more quickly.

✓ For the same reason, he sold his insulin patent to the University of Toronto for just one dollar.

✓ He treated diabetic patients for a fraction of the fee that other doctors were charging.

A friend said it would be impossible to rob Fred Banting, because he would happily give you everything he had in his pockets.

It's true that the discovery of insulin was a team effort. But the whole project had grown from one tiny seed. It had all started with FRED'S IDEA.

Question #2

Would you rather:

(a) take a sleeping pill?

(b) lie awake until 2:00 a.m. puzzling over an article you'd just read?

Fred's Answer:

"I prefer to think about the article, then get up and scribble my thoughts into a notebook."

Ah, here we are at the Aviation Museum. Pull your hat down over your ears, tug your scarf up over your nose and don't let go of Walter's leash. I'll wade through the drifts and you can walk in my footsteps.

On the evening of October 30, 1920, while Fred was preparing a lecture for medical students in London, Ontario, he read an article about diabetes. He tried to go to sleep, but the article was still whirling around in his head. The authors described how they had been trying — and failing — to isolate a certain substance in the pancreases of dogs. Lying there, unable to sleep, Fred suddenly thought of a way to do it. At 2:00 a.m. on Hallowe'en morning, he jumped out of bed and wrote in his notebook:

"Diabetus... [Fred was a terrible speller]*...*
Ligate pancreatic ducts of dogs. [Ooh! Please cover
Walter's ears!] *Keep dogs alive till acini degenerate*
leaving Islets. Try to isolate the
secretion of these to relieve glycosurea."
(Rough translation: "Start here.")

In fact, at that point Fred's idea was about as far from real insulin as we are from that big mysterious shape we can barely see through the snow. He travelled to Toronto three times before Dr. Macleod would take his idea seriously. But Fred simply did not give up.

Look up. That silver shape, which looms over us like a silent monster, is a Lockheed Hudson airplane, just like the one in which Fred took his last flight. You're seeing one of the last sights he ever saw.

Oh, dear. Even Walter looks sad! Let's trudge back through the snow to the taxi, and I'll cheer you up with an inspiring story about Fred's childhood.

Question #1
(The Last Question)

If you were walking home from school and saw two workers fall from a scaffold and get hurt, would you:

(a) stand there with your mouth hanging open?

(b) call 9-1-1?

Fred's Answer:

"Since 9-1-1 hasn't been invented yet, I'll run for help."

Fred did run for help. And when he stood watching the doctor treating those injured men, he decided right then and there to become a doctor, too. Millions of people the world over are very grateful that he did!

Just the Plain Facts about Frederick Banting

November 14, 1891

He was born in Alliston (now called New Tecumseth), Ontario, to William Thompson Banting and Margaret Grant Banting. He was the youngest of six children.

December 9, 1916

The day after he graduated from medical school he reported for military duty and was sent overseas with the Royal Canadian Army Medical Corps.

September 28, 1918

He was wounded during a battle in France, but stayed on the battlefield for twelve more hours, treating injured soldiers — and earning the Military Cross for his bravery.

June 1920

He tried to start a medical practice in London, Ontario, but few patients arrived and he had trouble making ends meet. He accepted a part-time teaching position at the university.

October 1920

While preparing for a lecture he got an idea about how diabetes might be treated.

May–Autumn 1921

In a laboratory at the University of Toronto, he and his assistant, Charles Best, showed that they could control diabetes in dogs. He and Best worked with Dr. Macleod and Dr. Collip to purify the extract.

January 1922

The first diabetic patient was successfully treated with insulin. Soon insulin was being produced and distributed from a lab in Toronto.

1922–1923

Banting won the Starr Gold Medal. Then he and Macleod won the Nobel Prize for Medicine. The Canadian government granted him an allowance of $7500 per year for life. He went to Buckingham Palace to meet King George V.

1923–1941

He conducted and supervised many experiments, especially in the fields of cancer research, ways to resuscitate drowning victims, and silicosis (a disease which affected the lungs of miners).

1924 He married Marion Robertson in Toronto; they divorced in 1932.

June 3, 1934

He was knighted and became Sir Frederick Banting.

June 1939

He married Henrietta Ball.

September 1, 1939
When World War II broke out he re-enlisted in the army. He did research on biological weapons, aviation medicine and the treatment of burns caused by mustard gas.

February 21, 1941
On his way from Newfoundland to England to discuss his research, he was killed in a plane crash.

1990 The crashed plane was airlifted to the Banting Memorial Interpretation Centre in Musgrave Harbour, Newfoundland.

2003 An eternal flame of hope is burning in front of the house in London, Ontario, where Banting first got his idea for insulin. When a cure for diabetes is finally found, the flame will be extinguished.

LIONEL CONACHER DOES IT ALL

Whoa! Did you see that? I almost fell headfirst into the boards! My feet keep trying to sneak away from the rest of me. Goodness, skating is not as easy as it looks!

Lionel Conacher suffered the same wobbles and oopses when he first stepped onto the rink here in Jesse Ketchum Park in Toronto. Most of his friends had learned how to skate when they were in kindergarten. But Lionel's family was too poor to buy sports equipment, so he didn't learn to skate until he was sixteen. Even so, he ended up playing in the NHL for twelve years — and hockey wasn't even his best sport!

Lionel Conacher wasn't just good at hockey. He was good at *everything*. Sometimes he hurried from one sporting event to another on the same day.

Once, at the Ontario baseball championships, he stepped up to the plate during the last inning. His team was losing by one run. But he swung the bat and whacked a beautiful double to centre field. Two of his teammates raced to home plate and won the game! Everyone cheered madly for Lionel Conacher, the hero! But where was he?

He was in a taxi, racing across town to join his lacrosse team, which was *also* in a battle for the Ontario championship. When he arrived at half-time, things were bad. His team was losing 3 to 0. He must have been at least a *little* tired after nine innings of baseball and a mad dash across town, but that didn't stop him. In the second half of the game he scored four goals and an assist. Thanks to him, the Maitlands won 5 to 3! He was the hero of two Ontario championship games, in *two* different sports, on the same day.

Lionel Conacher was big. He was strong. He was unstoppable. That's one reason why they called him The Big Train.

When The Big Train was only a Little Train, his family lived just down the road from here. There were a dozen people in his family — two parents and ten children, including two sets of twins — and they were very poor. Most of the children, including Lionel, dropped out of school after the eighth grade so they could help make ends meet.

Before that, Lionel attended Jesse Ketchum Public School, which is right here beside us. This used to be a tough neighbourhood, and the principal was worried that his students might get into trouble with the law. So he made a rule: every student at the school must join a team. Lionel's sisters competed in track-and-field and softball. His brothers played hockey and football. Lionel played *everything*: football, hockey, lacrosse, baseball, wrestling and boxing!

History does not record how he kept his calendar straight.

What was the secret of Lionel's success?
(1) He believed that the way to survive in a tough neighbourhood was to be a serious athlete.
(2) He loved sports more than anything else.
(3) He had a lot of physical energy.
(4) He was very talented.
(5) Frank Merriwell.

. . .*Whoops!* That ice is *hard*! Please help me up.

Frank Merriwell was the most handsome, brave and best-mannered person you could ever hope to meet. He went around saving people from burning buildings, catching bank robbers and scoring the winning touchdowns in college football games. He wasn't real, though — he was the hero of a series of books Lionel loved to read. When his football team was losing a playoff game, Lionel would hug the ball in a Frank-like manner, run like a big train (he could run 100 metres in 10 seconds) and bulldoze through the opposition. He wouldn't stop until he scored a touchdown.

Stop for a moment while I dig these sports cards out of my pocket.

★ LIONEL CONACHER ★

HT: 188 cm   WT: 86 kg   B: May 24, 1901   PH: 555-1212

YEAR	TEAM	LEAGUE	INTERESTING STUFF
1918–19	Century Rovers Aura Lee	Toronto Toronto	He played on both teams in the same season
1919–21	Toronto Canoe Club Paddlers	Ontario Juniors	Canadian Champions (Memorial Cup)
1922–23	North Toronto	Seniors	1st game ever broadcast on radio
1923–25	Pittsburgh Yellow Jackets	US Amateur Hockey Assn	Won the USAHA title two years in a row
1925–26	Pittsburgh Pirates	NHL	He scored the first goal in NHL franchise history
1926–30	NY Americans	NHL	
1930–32	Montreal Maroons	NHL	For 1930–31 he was voted Most Valuable Player on the team
1933–34	Chicago Black Hawks	NHL	Stanley Cup Champions He won a spot on the 1st NHL All-Star Team
1934–37	Montreal Maroons	NHL	Stanley Cup Champions

★ LIONEL CONACHER ★

| HT: 188 cm | WT: 86 kg | B: May 24, 1901 | PH: 555-1212 |

YEAR	TEAM	LEAGUE / INTERESTING STUFF	
1912–15	Toronto Capitals (tackle)	Toronto City League Rugby	Toronto Champions for 3 years in a row
1919	Toronto Capitals (halfback)	Ontario Rugby Football Union	Ontario Champions
1921	Toronto Argonauts (halfback)	Canadian Rugby Union	Grey Cup Champions
1922	Toronto Argonauts (captain)	Canadian Rugby Union	team was undefeated in regular season
1924–29	Duquesne University & Rutgers University (assistant coach)		
1933–34	Toronto Crosse & Blackwell Chefs (halfback/captain)	started the first professional football league in Canada	
1934–35	Wrigley Aromints (halfback/captain)	Crosse & Blackwell Chefs got a new sponsor and became the Aromints	

In 1922 he set a season record (scoring 33 singles) that stood for more than 60 years.

★ LIONEL CONACHER ★

| HT: 188 cm | WT: 86 kg | B: May 24, 1901 | PH: 555-1212 |

YEAR	SPORT	INTERESTING STUFF
1916	Wrestling	Ontario Champion in the 57-kilo (125-lb.) category
1920	Baseball	Ontario Championship
1920	Boxing	Canadian light-heavyweight champion
1921	Boxing	boxed a 4-round exhibition with Jack Dempsey (world heavyweight champion)
1922	Lacrosse	Ontario Champions
1922	Baseball	declined an offer to turn professional
1926	Baseball	Triple-A Champions and Little World Series champs
1931	Lacrosse	won the scoring title (107 points)
1932	Pro Wrestling	undefeated in the season (26 matches)

In 1950 the Canadian Press voted him Canada's Athlete of the Century. He won 33 votes. The runner-up won 2.

As you know, trading cards usually feature athletes who are good at one sport. But Lionel Conacher was good at so many things, I had to design that special set of cards just to help you keep track of his career. While we're skating, I'll tell you some other interesting facts. For example, The Big Train was scared to death of his dentist!

In sports, "professional" means an athlete who is paid to compete. But if Lionel became a professional in one sport, he would not be allowed to compete in the others. So he turned down two big offers from NHL teams and "worked" instead at a clothing store and a dry-cleaning business. The stores were happy to use his famous name and face to attract customers.

If you ask your favourite adult who Lionel Conacher was, he or she will probably say, "Who?", "I don't know," or "Aren't you supposed to be walking the dog?" Not many people remember him today. But during the 1920s and 1930s he was a superhero sports star — everything he touched turned to gold. Every team he joined was a winner. But Lionel felt something was missing. He wanted an education. So in 1923, when he won an academic scholarship to an American prep school, he packed his bags, said goodbye to his (many) teammates and moved to Pittsburgh.

American sports fans were thrilled! Canadians were devastated! And one seventeen-year-old girl named Dorothy had a special reason to bawl her eyes out. She had been married to The Big Train for only a couple of weeks when he hurried away to the States, leaving her in Toronto to finish her own education. To make matters worse, she and Lionel ran away and got married without permission, and her parents were furious. Her father wouldn't even speak to him. That must have been a lonely time for all of them.

Lionel was older than the other students at Bellefonte Academy, and he missed his wife, but he worked hard at his studies and played brilliantly on the football and hockey teams. In November of 1925 he finally took the plunge into professional sports. When his amateur team (the Pittsburgh Yellow Jackets) became an NHL expansion team called the Pittsburgh Pirates, he signed up with them. Two weeks later he scored the first goal in the Pirates' franchise history. Then he scored twenty-eight goals in twenty-nine games. By the end of the season he had the highest score in the league — eighty-seven points — and he wasn't even a forward! (He played left defence.) Everywhere he went, fans mobbed and congratulated him.

Watch me do a spin! *CRASH! Ooof* . . .

When a person starts to think he's invincible, sometimes a big crash comes and knocks the wind right out of him. That's what happened to Lionel Conacher. I'll just lie here on the ice while I tell you about it.

Lionel didn't fall on the rink. He took a different sort of tumble. He started to drink a lot of alcohol. His hockey-playing got worse and worse, he was traded from the New York Americans to the Montreal Maroons, and the next thing he knew he was on waivers, which meant he would be sold to the first team that made an offer. Lionel's life began to fall apart.

Sometimes people die from their addictions. Luckily, Lionel didn't. Being put on waivers was a wake-up call for him, and it was quickly followed by another. On November 25,

1930, he became a father, and when he saw tiny baby Constance he finally vowed to break his addiction. As Frank Merriwell would have done, he put every bit of his tremendous strength into keeping that promise.

But it was a nightmare year. He struggled against the intense craving for alcohol by filling up on chocolate, soft drinks and tea. He played round after round of golf. He took up pipe smoking. And he went to the movies. He couldn't sit still long enough to see the whole show, so when his restless energy forced him to leave he would look at his watch. The next day he would come back at that time to see the rest of the movie. When he had been sober for eight months, he came down with pneumonia. He lay sick in bed for weeks. And when he recovered from *that*, he developed a tumour and had to have an operation. What an awful year it was!

If you look at the sports cards I gave you, you'll see what happened in 1931 when he beat his addiction. He went back to his teams with new courage and determination. Not only did the Maroons* take him off waivers, they voted him Most Valuable Player. He also became the top scorer in the lacrosse league, scoring 107 points — almost twice as many as the runner-up.

During the summer he played professional football. He took up wrestling again — and went undefeated for a whole season. He was definitely back in stride.

By the time he recovered from his terrible year, his

Footnote: By the way, his lacrosse team and his hockey team were both called The Montreal Maroons. I wonder if he ever got them mixed up on his calendar?

younger brother Charlie had joined the Toronto Maple Leafs. Hockey fans loved the rivalry between them. One time they started fighting on the ice and kept going all the way to the edge of the rink, up the ramp and out to the lobby, where Charlie finally surrendered. (History doesn't record what their mother thought of this disgraceful behaviour.) But most of the time Lionel and Charlie got along very well, and sometimes they would do a little crowd pleasing. Once, in the penalty box, they started gesturing angrily. To the fans it looked as if they were having a big argument, but really Lionel was growling, "How are Mom and Dad doing today?" and Charlie was sneering back "They're fine," and shaking his fist. It was all for show.

In 1935 Lionel and Charlie opened their own gas station at the corner of Yonge Street and Davenport Road in Toronto. It was one way a retiring hockey player could continue to make a good living, and Lionel — whose family was growing — was looking toward the future.

On April 23, 1937, he played his last professional hockey game. After twelve years in the NHL he must have been a little tired. And as you can see from the special bonus trading card on the right, he had also been knocked around a teeny bit:

OFFICIAL OUCH FACTS

★ LIONEL CONACHER ★

| Height: Ow | Weight: Ouch | Comment: Waaahhh! |

NUMBER	BODY PART	TYPE OF INJURY
8 times	nose bone	broken
once	arm bone	broken
once	leg bone	broken
several	hand bones	broken
10	ribs	cracked
16 stitches	jugular vein	gashed — nearly died
1 serious	thigh	gash
500 stitches	face and head	various cuts and slashes
100 stitches	everywhere	various wounds and gashes
2 times	knee	cartilage damaged
too many	everywhere	sprains, strains, bruises, black eyes

🕊 **Official Ouch Facts** 🕊

But here's a strange fact: after surviving all those gashes, crashes and close calls, Lionel Conacher finally died of something totally unexpected. After he retired from sports, he was elected to the Ontario legislature in 1937, then to the federal parliament in 1949. One day, when he and some other politicians were playing a charity softball game on the lawn of Parliament Hill in Ottawa, Lionel smacked a terrific triple. He began to run the bases in his usual unstoppable style. But he never made it back to home plate. His great big heart gave out. He collapsed and died of a heart attack right there on the field. He was only fifty-three years old.

But he left us a beautiful legacy. As a politician, his special goal was to build more parks and recreation centres, swimming pools, basketball courts, gyms and ice rinks. He knew sports could change a kid's life, and he wanted every kid to have a chance to play, just as he had.

What can we do to salute him? Let's stop right here on the rink behind Jesse Ketchum School and look up at the snowy sky. Do you think we can do a beautiful spin, all of us together? One, two, three . . . TAH-DAH!

Just the Plain Facts about Lionel Conacher

May 24, 1900
Lionel Pretoria Conacher was born to Benjamin Conacher and Elizabeth (Black) Conacher. He had nine brothers and sisters.

1912–1915
His junior football team won the Toronto championship three years in a row.

1916 He learned to skate and played on two Toronto hockey teams, and won the 125-lb. (57-kilo) wrestling championship of Ontario.

1919 His football team won the Ontario championship and his hockey team won the Canadian championship.

1920 He won the Canadian light-heavyweight boxing championship.

1921 He joined the Toronto Argonauts football team, which won the Grey Cup. He also boxed a four-round exhibition bout with world heavyweight champion Jack Dempsey.

1922 His lacrosse team won the senior Ontario championship. His football team, the Toronto Argonauts, went undefeated in the regular season. He turned down offers to play professional hockey for the Montréal Canadiens and professional baseball for a Toronto team.

1923 He married Dorothy Kennedy; over the years, they had five children (Constance, Diane, Lionel Junior, Brian and David). He attended Bellefonte Academy in Pittsburgh.

1925 He accepted an offer to play professional hockey in Pittsburgh.

1926 His baseball team won the AAA and Little World Series championships. He was traded from the Pittsburgh Pirates hockey team to the New York Americans.

1927–30
He was an assistant football coach at Rutgers University, then a player-coach for the New York Americans hockey team.

1930–31
He was traded to the Montreal Maroons hockey team, which put him on waivers. After his first daughter was born, he overcame a drinking problem and serious illness.

1931 He was voted Most Valuable Player by the Montreal Maroons hockey team, and was top-scorer on an international lacrosse team *also* called the Montreal Maroons.

1932 He was undefeated in a season of professional wrestling (twenty-six matches).

1933 He was both captain and halfback on a pro football team in Toronto, and played for the Chicago Black Hawks hockey team, which won the Stanley Cup.

1934 His hockey team, the Montreal Maroons, won the Stanley Cup. He wrote a regular column about football for the *Toronto Telegram* newspaper.

1935–38
With his brother Charlie, he opened a service station in Toronto. He retired from hockey and was elected to the Ontario parliament. Later he became the athletic commissioner for the province of Ontario.

1939 During World War II he set up a Canadian sports program for the armed services.

1949 He was elected to the federal parliament.

1950 The Canadian Press voted him Canada's Athlete of the Half-Century.

May 26, 1954
He died suddenly of a heart attack while playing in a charity softball game.

1955–1994
He was inducted into the Canadian Sports Hall of Fame, the Canadian Football Hall of Fame, the Canadian Lacrosse Hall of Fame and Museum, and the Hockey Hall of Fame.

2000 He came fourth in a poll to name Canada's Athlete of the Century.

Now The Lionel Conacher Award is given annually to the Canadian Male Athlete of the Year.

"ROCKET" RICHARD: HOW TO BE A SUPERSTAR

Please exit the taxi onto the sidewalk, not into the cobblestone street, where a car or a horse might crash into you. Join me on the steps in front of Notre Dame Cathedral. Montreal is one of the oldest cities in Canada, and this is one of the oldest places in Montreal. But I want to tell you about something that happened here recently. On May 31, 2000, a hearse pulled up at the bottom of these steps. Three thousand people — family, friends, teammates and special guests like the mayor of Montreal, the Premier of Quebec and the Prime Minister of Canada — were waiting to say goodbye to one of the greatest hockey players who ever lived. As his coffin was carried up the steps, people started to clap.

No, they were not clapping because he was dead. They did it as a tribute, a way to say thank you. His name was Maurice Richard, and everyone called him The Rocket. To many Canadians he was a legend. And to French Canadians he was even more than that. The Rocket showed them how to be fighters and winners. When he died, they stood in this square and wept. (Please pass me a tissue. It's so cold that the tears are freezing on my eyelashes.) Like Maurice Richard, you too might accidentally become a superstar, and it's always a good idea to be prepared for such things.

SUPERSTAR-IN-TRAINING RULE #1

KEEP YOUR EYE ON THE PUCK

When people were cheering and calling the Rocket a marvel, a hero, a legend, he thought only about how to score the next goal. He was called the "greatest hockey player who ever lived," yet he regularly arrived on the ice earlier and stayed later than the other players, practising his shots on the empty rink. He helped his team to win the Stanley Cup eight times. When he retired, he held the records for the most regular season goals (544), the most playoff goals (82), the most hat-tricks (33), and the most winning goals (101). He was a member of the Hockey Hall of Fame, the Canadian Sports Hall of Fame, and the Temple de la Renommée du Sport du Québec. He received the Order of Canada, the Ordre nationale du Québec and the Hart Trophy. But The Rocket said, "I am just a hockey player."

After he died, his body lay in state at the Molson Centre, which is the present home of the Montréal Canadiens hockey team. But that's not where he dazzled his opponents and his fans. He played at the old Montréal Forum. As we drive over there, would you please study the following list?

Words Used to Describe
Maurice "Rocket" Richard

On the Ice: exciting, thrilling, lightning-quick, strong, brilliant, unstoppable

Off the Ice/In the Dressing Room: silent, intense, shy, unassuming, brooding, taciturn

In the French Newspapers: *explosif, flamboyant, une merveille physique, l'idole d'un peuple, la crème de la crème, le Babe Ruth du Hockey*

In the English Newspapers: explosive, passionate, a mad dog in a savage quest for goals, a hero for Quebec, the Babe Ruth of Hockey

In front of a Cheering Crowd: modest, shy, embarrassed, nervous, awkward, bashful

With his Family: relaxed, attentive, devoted, a family man, a good father

SUPERSTAR-IN-TRAINING RULE #2

BE KIND TO CHILDREN AND OTHER PEOPLE

When Maurice Richard was a new player with the Canadiens, he timidly asked his favourite Maple Leafs hockey player for an autograph. But the player said No! It was such a painful moment that Maurice remembered it for the rest of his life. He vowed never to treat anyone that way, and he never did.

He was a shy kid who loved hockey so much he sometimes wore his skates all day long. He played hockey on the icy road, at the local rinks and even (but you must promise never to do this, because it is extremely dangerous) on the frozen edges of the river.

SUPERSTAR-IN-TRAINING RULE #3

BE PASSIONATE

He only stopped playing hockey long enough for dinner, and even then he sometimes kept his skates on. After dinner he clomped back outside to practise stick-handling, shooting and skating. All day he thought about hockey, and at night he lay in bed dreaming up new plays and new angles.

Maybe you're saying to yourself, "If I were a hockey genius like Maurice Richard, I would be passionate about it, too." (Are you saying that?) Well, here's a surprise for you: at first, he was awful. He was small for his age, the bigger players would rough him up, and he could hardly ever get the puck. When he played for his school teams, and later when he played junior hockey in the local leagues, he seemed awkward on the ice (and off it!). But he *loved* the game. He practised and practised and practised. Finally, people started to notice him:

Visiting Players: Who is that guy scoring all the goals?

Hockey Scouts/Agents: Who is that guy scoring all the goals?

Coach (Georges Norchet): Mmm, Richard is scoring a lot of goals.

Lucille Norchet (Georges' sister): Who is that guy scoring all the goals?

Maurice was invited to the Senior Canadiens training camp. He was a good player, a passionate player. He could skate like lightning. But suddenly he had another problem, and it sounded like this: *snap!*

Maurice Richard's Early Career
The Plumley Norris Cold-and-Factual Version™

September 1940
In his very first game at the Senior Canadiens training camp he broke his ankle and was unable to play for the rest of the season.

September 1941
In his second season at the Senior Canadiens training camp he fell against the goalpost and broke his wrist. He missed the whole year except the playoffs.

December 27, 1942
During his first season with the NHL Montréal Canadiens he crashed into the boards and broke his right ankle. He did not play for the rest of the season.

Another player might have given up. But not Mr. Brittle Bones. I mean, Maurice.

SUPERSTAR-IN-TRAINING RULE #4

DON'T QUIT

Maurice must have wondered whether his bones were too fragile for the NHL. Everyone *else* was certainly wondering, especially coaches and sportswriters. But after each injury he trained hard and returned to the ice in record time. He was determined to prove to himself and everyone else that he belonged on the team.

Here we are in the taxi queue beside Atwater Park. These days, the building across the road is a glitzy warehouse full of arcade games, movie theatres and other money-making amusements. But for seventy-one years the Montreal Forum was a magical place for hockey fans. For Maurice, it was a home away from home.

In spite of his injuries, good things were happening. In September of 1942 he and Lucille got married. A few weeks later, on Hallowe'en night, he played his first NHL hockey game. A week after that he scored his first goal, right here at the Forum. It would be the first of many, many, many goals: 626 of them, to be exact.

SUPERSTAR-IN-TRAINING RULE #5

WORK HARD

How to Work Hard —
The Rocket Richard Way

Which of the following would you prefer?

(a) Have a huge defenceman named Earl Siebert jump on your back and hang on, dragging his skates along the ice. Skate another 20 metres like that and score a goal.

(b) Get knocked out in the seventh game of the Stanley Cup semi-finals. Go and get six stitches in your head. Stagger back and ask the coach what the score is. When he says, "We're tied, one-all," immediately forget. Even though your eyes are blurry and you can't remember where you are, tell him you want to play. Stumble onto the ice. Hook the puck from behind the goal and find a tiny opening among the clattering hockey sticks. Fire the puck into the net, winning the game and earning your team a spot in the finals. Make your way to the dressing room, where your father is waiting to see if you are all right. Fall into his arms, sobbing hysterically, and go into convulsions. Later, some people will call this

THE GOAL OF THE CENTURY.

(Plumley Norris Safety Note: never do either of these things in real life.)

SUPERSTAR-IN-TRAINING RULE #6

EXPECT TROUBLE

The better Maurice played, the harder the other teams tried to stop him. They assigned one player (sometimes *two*) to slow him down — to block him, check him, hound him and make his life miserable. I wish I could tell you that he endured their attacks calmly and with great dignity, never hitting back.

Yes, I certainly wish I could tell you that.

The other players grabbed him. They punched him. They hooked him with their sticks, hammered him into the boards, tripped him and called him dirty names. The Rocket would endure this treatment for a while, but when he hit the boiling point he would explode.

Then he was terrifying, with fists like rocks and a mouth like a firecracker. Sometimes he'd pulverize his attacker and then turn on the linesmen. During his career he spent the equivalent of twenty-four whole games in the penalty box. On March 13, 1955, an opponent clobbered Maurice over the head with his stick. OW!

The blow opened a wound that would need eight stitches. Maurice retaliated. Three times the linesman took away the stick he was using as a weapon. Three times Maurice grabbed another stick and kept fighting. Finally the linesman jumped him from behind and wrestled him to the ice.

Wham! Wham! Maurice punched him in the face. Twice. *OW! OW!* (**Note:** I'm not recommending this sort of behaviour. I'm just *telling* you about it.)

This was not the first time The Rocket had fought with game officials. He'd paid stiff fines for similar incidents in the past. But this time, when NHL president Clarence Campbell announced The Rocket's punishment, Montrealers couldn't believe their ears. He was suspended for the rest of the season, *including the playoffs.* He would lose his rank as the top points scorer in the NHL. And without him the team didn't stand a chance at the Stanley Cup.

Not fair! shouted the fans, the radio stations, the newspapers. Too harsh! Was The Rocket being punished so severely because he was French Canadian? The French Canadians thought so. The mayor of Montreal demanded justice. A member of parliament tried to debate the suspension in the House of Commons and was ruled out of order. Here comes THE BiG TROUBLE.

Superstar-in-Training Rules for Emergency Situations

A Plumley Norris Special Edition Quiz™

It's not always the superstar's fault when fans behave badly. However, the superstar can sometimes make things better by behaving wisely. Could you handle the Richard Riot as well as The Rocket did?

1. **The Emergency Situation Begins:**
   Tension in the city grew and grew. Death threats were made against Clarence Campbell. People (silly people, I mean) boycotted Campbell's Soup just because it shared his name. As game time approached, crowds gathered in front of the Forum. The sidewalks bristled with people and picket signs. Extra police were on duty.

In a situation like this, you should:

(a) quietly and inconspicuously enter the Forum and slip into your seat

(b) grab a loudspeaker and shout: "LADIES AND GENTLEMEN! THE SUPERSTAR HAS ENTERED THE BUILDING!"

2. **The Emergency Situation Continues:**
   Inside the Forum, the Canadiens were trailing 2 to 0. Even though Maurice and his wife had entered quietly, the crowd noticed them and cheered loudly. But at the

end of the first period when Clarence Campbell and his fiancée came in and sat down, an ugly hush fell over the crowd. Then voices began to shout. *Shoo, Campbell! Vive Richard!* Campbell ignored them. They pelted him with garbage, hot dogs, overshoes, ice cubes, programs and eggs. He sat calmly and watched the game. Montréal was now behind 4 to 0.

This would be a good time for the superstar to:

(a) stand up and bellow, "Take that, you BOZO!"

(b) shout, "Can I get some popcorn over here?"

(c) sit quietly and stay alert in case of danger

3. **A Crisis:**
   During the intermission, a man smashed two tomatoes into Campbell's chest. A moment later a tear-gas bomb exploded, thrown by an angry fan. The air filled with thick yellow smoke, and the crowd began to struggle toward the exits, gasping and blinded by fumes. People poured out onto the street where the angry mob had been loitering for hours.

As a superstar, you should now:

(a) walk up to a choking fan and ask, "Do you know who I am?"

(b) quietly give your spouse the pre-arranged signal to leave the building, then do so in an orderly fashion

4. **The Last Straw:**
   The Forum was still full of tear-gas. Campbell was whisked away from the danger. The Rocket and his wife were smuggled out a side door to a waiting car. The fire chief considered the options carefully. Then he

shook his head: it wasn't safe to continue. He would have to close the building. The Canadiens were forced to forfeit the game to Detroit.

That was the last straw. The crowd went berserk. Bottles smashed. Windows shattered. Cars burned. People ran up and down the street, screaming and wrecking anything they could get their hands on.

At this point, the superstar (you!) ought to:

(a) start shrieking, waving your arms, running around, and bumping into things

(b) slip out the side door to a waiting car

(c) go home.

(d) (b) and (c)

(e) all of the above

5. Aftermath:

By 3 a.m. the streets were covered with garbage and broken glass. Seventy of the worst troublemakers were taken to the police station. By some miracle, nobody had been killed or badly hurt. The next morning Montrealers woke up to $100,000 worth of damage. The Rocket was asked to go on the radio and make a public statement.

In the aftermath of the worst sports riot in Canadian history, it is a good idea for a superstar to go on the radio and say:

(a) "I suppose you're wondering why I called you all here today."

(b) "Did you hear the one about the Zamboni driver and the pizza?"

(c) that it hurts you to be out of the playoffs, but that you
     accept your punishment and hope the fans will get out
     there and support the team, then promise to come
     back the next year and help win the Stanley Cup

Compare your answers to Maurice Richard's (at the end of the
chapter).

ΟΟΟΟΟ

All summer Maurice trained hard and threw himself
eagerly into the new season. His coach advised him to hammer the puck into the net instead of hammering the bullies:
"Don't get mad. Get even." So Maurice struggled to control
his temper. It was hard. But it worked. The Rocket stayed on
the ice and the Canadiens won the Stanley Cup *five years in
a row.*

SUPERSTAR-IN-TRAINING RULE #7

SUCCESS IS THE BEST REVENGE

Late in his career The Rocket began to suffer injuries again, and he gained weight. He felt he was moving more and more slowly on the ice. A slow Rocket was still faster than almost any other player in the league, but after 18 NHL seasons and 1111 games he began to think about retiring. When he announced his decision in September of 1960, the whole country mourned. It was truly the end of an era.

SUPERSTAR-IN-TRAINING RULE #8

ENJOY BEING A KID

Play hard. Throw your whole heart into the things you love, and never mind what other people think of you. Then, if you accidentally grow up to be a superstar, you can tell fans and other bright young people: "When I was a kid, I was *just like you.*"

Answers to the Plumley Norris Special Edition Quiz: 1-a, 2-c, 3-b, 4-d, 5-c.

Just the Plain Facts
about Maurice Richard

August 4, 1921

He was born in Montreal, Quebec, to Onésime and Alice Richard.

1939–1942

He played for the Paquette team in the Parc Lafontaine Juvenile League, and for the Verdun Juniors from 1939–1940.

September 1940

He was invited to the Senior Canadiens training camp; in his first game, he broke his ankle.

June 1941

He was rejected for military service because of his broken ankle.

September 1941

He returned to the Senior Canadiens training camp, but broke his wrist. He returned in time for the playoffs, and scored six goals. The Montréal

Canadiens signed him up.

September 21, 1942
He married Lucille Norchet. Over the years, they had seven children (Huguette, Maurice Jr., Normand, André, Suzanne, Paul and Jean).

October 31, 1942
He played his first game with the Montréal Canadiens.

March 18, 1945
He was the first NHL player to score fifty goals in fifty games.

March 16, 1955
When NHL president Clarence Campbell suspended him because he punched a linesman, a riot broke out in Montreal.

September 1955
Maurice's younger brother Henri joined the Canadiens. His nickname was The Pocket Rocket.

April 10, 1956
The Canadiens won their eighth Stanley Cup. Maurice scored the winning goal.

October 19, 1957
He was the first NHL player to score 500 goals.

November 13, 1957
A player's skate cut the back of his leg and severed his Achilles tendon. He missed forty-two games.

January 1958
He broke his ankle again. The Canadiens won the Stanley Cup, but The Rocket was able to play only a few shifts.

Late November 1959
A puck hit him in the face and broke his cheekbone; he missed nineteen games.

April 14, 1960

The Montréal Canadiens won the Stanley Cup in the fourth game of the finals. It was Richard's last NHL game.

September 15, 1960

He announced his retirement after 1111 games.

October 6, 1960

In his honour, Canadiens sweater #9 was retired.

June 1961

He was inducted into the Hockey Hall of Fame.

November 24, 1967

He was one of the first people to receive the Order of Canada.

1985 He became an officer of the Ordre national du Québec.

July 18, 1994

His wife Lucille died of cancer.

March 11, 1996

The Montreal Forum closed its doors after seventy-one years. During the closing ceremonies Maurice Richard received a ten-minute standing ovation from the crowd.

October 22, 1998

He was promoted from Order of Canada to Companion of the Order of Canada by the Governor-General.

1999 The Maurice "Rocket" Richard Trophy was created. It is presented each year to the top goal-scorer in the NHL.

May 27, 2000

He died of cancer in Montreal. His funeral took place on May 31.

THE POST & MAIL NEWSPAPER

January 30, 1997

Prof Pays the Price Over Brock Blunder

Sir Issac Brock's famous hat

OTTAWA — After a blunder which left his reputation in ruins, the eminent Canadian historian Dr. Plumley Q. Norris resigned yesterday from his position with the Extremely Important Institute of Canadian Studies (EIICS). Last month, Norris startled viewers of the national news show "This Is the News" by twice referring to the famous British general, Sir Isaac Brock, as Mr. Big-Head.

The professor's first slip-up occurred when Norris remarked that the Battle of Queenston Heights was "marred by the death of Mr. Big-Head." He giggled and apologized, explaining that he sometimes assigns "little made-up names" to historical figures "so I can remember them better." But forty-seven seconds later Norris repeated the blunder, asking viewers to imagine

A-4

"what might have happened if Mr. Big-Head had lived longer."

The flustered professor then tried to justify his error by demonstrating the large size of Brock's skull. First he twisted his bow-tie around his head, but was apparently unable to remove it. Then he measured the circumference of a metal wastebasket, placed it upside down over his head, and continued his lecture. Executive producer Toni-Jack Jenningsley said, "It was great. He sounded exactly like Darth Vader."

Norris's colleague, Dr. Lois Williams, said, "He's been studying Brock's hat for two whole years. He just finished a paper about the brim and he was starting on the ostrich feathers. People don't realize how stressful this kind of research can be."

Brock ordered the cocked hat from England, but was killed during the War of 1812 before had a chance to wear it.

When questioned about his blunder, Norris would say only, "Sixty-three centimetres is extremely large, even for the twenty-first century skull." He declined to comment on his resignation, or to confirm rumours that he has been hired to drive a cab for a local taxi company.

FAMOUS PORTRAIT GALLERY

Famous Dead Canadians speak out — the Plumley Norris version

I'm telling you the truth. Honest.

Madeleine de Verchères

Samuel de Champlain

I wish someone would invent the life jacket.

Simon Fraser

Laura Secord

John Ware

Tecumseh

189

L.M. Montgomery

Louis Cyr

Frederick Banting

Billy Bishop

Lionel Conacher

Rocket Richard

Illustration Credits

Samuel de Champlain
p. 12: Théophile Hamel, *Samuel de Champlain* (detail), National Archives of Canada C-14305.
p. 187 lower: John Henry de Rinzy, *Champlain in an Indian Canoe*, National Archives of Canada C-013320.

Madeleine de Verchères
p. 24: Wartime Recruiting Poster "Madeleine de Vercheres, 1648–1747, Hier, Aujourd'hui" (detail), Canadian War Museum, 56-05-12-139.
p. 187 upper: Gerald S. Hayward, *Marie Madeleine de Verchères*, National Archives of Canada C-083513.

Simon Fraser
p. 42: *Simon Fraser, 1776–1862, Fur Trader* (detail). British Columbia Archives, PDP02258.
p. 188 upper: Charles William Jefferys, *Simon Fraser Descending the Fraser River*, National Archives of Canada C-070270.

Laura Secord
p. 57: *Laura Secord* [wood engraving], National Archives of Canada C-010717.
p. 188 lower: Lorne Kidd Smith, *Meeting Between Laura Secord and Lieut. Fitzgibbon, June 1813,* National Archives of Canada C-011053.

Tecumseh
p. 74: *Imaginary portrait of Tecumseh*, from "Tecumseh, a Drama," by Charles Mair, National Archives of Canada C-000319.
p. 189 lower left: Charles William Jefferys, *Meeting of Brock and Tecumseh, 1812*, National Archives of Canada C-073719.
p. 189 lower right: Frederick H. Brigden, *Tecumseh* (1768–1813), National Archives of Canada C-016744.

John Ware
p. 89: *John Ware, Rancher* (detail), Glenbow Archives, NA-101-37 (detail of NA-156-10).
p. 189 upper: *John Ware and his dog Bismark*, Glenbow Archives, NA-266-5.

Illustration Credits

Louis Cyr
p. 103: *Louis Cyr* (detail), National Archives of Canada C-086343.
p. 190 lower: *Louis Cyr Challenged by the Marquess of Queensberry to resist the opposing pull of two of Queensberry's dapple greys in England*, National Archives of Canada PA-209767.

Lucy Maud Montgomery
p. 119: L.M. Montgomery (detail), L.M. Montgomery Collections, Archival and Special Collections, University of Guelph Library.
p. 190 upper: *Lucy Maud Montgomery at age 14,* L.M. Montgomery Collections, Archival and Special Collections, University of Guelph Library.

Billy Bishop
p. 135: *Billy Bishop in his S.E 5a fighter* (detail), William Rider-Rider/National Archives of Canada PA-001654.
p. 191 lower: National Archives of Canada C-3541.

Sir Frederick Banting
p. 150: *Dr. Frederick Banting, [ca. 1940]* (detail), Archives of Ontario, F-9-3-4-1.
p. 191 upper: Thomas Fisher Rare Book Library, University of Toronto 10005400.

Lionel Conacher
p. 192 lower right: Hockey Hall of Fame #0073.
p. 192 upper: "New York Americans" runner up, National Hockey League 1928–1929, National Archives of Canada PA-194592.
p. 165 (detail) and p.192 lower left: Football Hall of Fame and Museum.

Maurice Richard
p. 182 (detail) and p. 193: Imperial Oil-Turofsky/Hockey Hall of Fame.
p. 193 lower: "Maurice Richard 'The Rocket,' hockey player, holding three pucks and a hat representing his goal production for a game between the Montréal Canadiens and the Chicago Black Hawks," National Archives of Canada PA-209768, copyright Southam/*The Gazette*, Montreal. Photo by Paul Taillefer.

Sir Isaac Brock's Hat
p. 185: Courtesy of Niagara Historical Society & Museum.

Selected Bibliography

Berton, Pierre. *Pierre Berton's Canada: the Land and the People.* North York, ON: Stoddart, 1999.

Canada Heirloom [series]. Mississauga, ON: Heirloom Publishing, 1998.

Canadian Encyclopedia. *100 Canadian Originals.* Historica Foundation of Canada, 2002.

Canadians All: Portraits of our People. [8 vols.] Toronto: Methuen, 1979–1989.

Ford, Karen and Janet MacLean and Barry Wansbrough. *Great Canadian Lives: Portraits in Heroism to 1867.* Scarborough, ON: Nelson, 1985.

Gillmor, Don et al. *Canada: A People's History.* [2 vols.] Toronto: McClelland and Stewart, 2000–2001.

Hacker, Carlotta. *The Book of Canadians: an Illustrated Guide to Who Did What.* Edmonton: Hurtig, 1983.

Hancock, Pat. *The Penguin Book of Canadian Biography for Young Readers: Early Canada.* Toronto: Penguin Books, 1999.

Hehner, Barbara. *The Penguin Book of Canadian Biography for Young Readers, Vol. 2, 1867–1945.* Toronto: Penguin, 2002.

Horizon Canada: A New Way to Discover the History of Canada. [10 vols.] Laval, PQ: Centre for the Study of Teaching Canada, 1987.

National Library of Canada. *Memorable Canadians.* Updated online January 24, 2002.

Joanne Stanbridge can't get enough of books. A reference librarian by day, she says the funniest reference question she has ever had was: "I need a book about poison ivy. *Fast*." When she's not answering reference questions, Joanne writes and illustrates. Her first novel, *The Leftover Kid*, about a girl who's adopted by the Prime Minister, was shortlisted for the Red Cedar Award. The picture book she illustrated, *My Four Lions* (by Bernice Gold), was named an Ontario Library Association Best Bet for 1999. Joanne is currently at work on a book about Mabel Bell, wife of famed inventor Alexander Graham Bell, "and a totally cool person in her own right." Joanne lives in Kingston, Ontario.

Bill Dickson's madcap illustrations romp across the pages of *First Folks and Vile Voyageurs, Made in Canada, The Scholastic Teacher's Diary* and the cover of *Why Did the Underwear Cross the Road?* Bill lives just a stone's throw away from beautiful Sauble Beach, Ontario, with his wife Eeva and their dog.